Stephen Georgeson Hatherly

A Treatise on Byzantine Music

Stephen Georgeson Hatherly

A Treatise on Byzantine Music

ISBN/EAN: 9783337084516

Printed in Europe, USA, Canada, Australia, Japan

Cover: Foto ©Thomas Meinert / pixelio.de

More available books at **www.hansebooks.com**

BY THE VERY REV.

S. G. HATHERLEY, Mus. Bac. Oxon.

PROTOPRESBYTER OF THE PATRIARCHAL ŒCUMENICAL THRONE OF CONSTANTINOPLE

LONDON
SOLD BY WILLIAM REEVES
83 CHARING CROSS ROAD, W.C.

PREFACE.

This work has to do with results rather than processes. It is not a Grammar of music, or so-called "theory;" still less is it a Method of musical composition. It is the amplification and completion of an effort made for the first time in English in the pages of *The Scottish Review* * to clear up some of the difficulties which beset the student when confronted with Eastern music generally.† Reasoning from what is better known to that which is less known, after discussing the formation of the musical scale, it passes in review the Gregorian system, a Western development of Eastern tradition, and proceeds to a full description of the old Greek diatonic genus, the chromatic genus, and the mixture of the diatonic and chromatic on which the bulk of Eastern music, now prevalent, is constructed. There are upwards of fifty unabbreviated musical pieces, ancient and modern, from Greek, Russian, Turkish, and Egyptian sources, given and fully analyzed: the way thereby being opened up for future musical composers who may desire to cultivate this vast and fertile, but hitherto unknown and unexplored musical field. Incidental proof is also offered of the Eastern origin of several of the supposed novelties in current Western music of the most advanced type. ‡

The student is requested, in perusing the work, to pass by no remark until its meaning is thoroughly comprehended. Also, excepting the fundamental 2 : 3 first principle of paragraph 8, on which the whole fabric is based, he is requested to take no single calculation for granted, but to verify each and all for himself. It will perhaps be found an advantage to read first the *Summary* in Part VI., and refer back to the different paragraphs as marked therein.

A learned friend and great traveller, who it was hoped would have furnished an Introduction on the history of Byzantine art in its various branches, has, through ill-health and multiplicity of engagements, been obliged to decline the task. This is a cause of regret to the writer, with which his readers would fully sympathise could they guage the extent of the loss sustained.

S. G. H.

Egremont, Cheshire, March, 1892.

---

* Vol. XIV., October 1889, pages 239-280.

† This phrase, "Eastern music generally," must be construed within the limits of the title-word *Byzantine*, and be applied to the nations under the influence of the Eastern Roman Empire. The nations of the ultra-orient, India, China, and Japan, "the East" of to-day, are not included.

‡ See paragraphs 89, 107, 325, etc.

CONTENTS.

PART   I. Preliminary

PART   II. The Diatonic Genus

PART   III. The Chromatic Genus

PART   IV. Classification of Scales

PART   V. Application and Specimens

PART   VI. Summary and Conclusion

vi

LIST OF MUSICAL SPECIMENS ANALYSED.

	PAGE
A Cradle Song, of Smyrna (*Hyper Chromatic Hypodorian*)	125
A Desponding-Complainer's Song, of Smyrna (*Pure Chromatic; and co-normal form of Hyper Chromatic Hypodorian*)	131
A Disappointed-Lover's Song, of Smyrna (*Hyper Chromatic Hypodorian*)	127
A Lover's Song, of Smyrna (*Dorian*)	84
A Lover's Song, of Smyrna (*Phrygian*)	92
A Lover's Song, of Smyrna (*Pseudo-Hypophrygian, A.; and Mixolydian*)	107
A Lover's Song, of Smyrna (*Hyper Chromatic Lydian; and Lydian*)	133
A Nautical Song, of Smyrna (*Lydian; and Pure Chromatic*)	123
A Parting Song, of Smyrna (*Hypophrygian*)	96
A Parting Song, of Smyrna (*Chromatic Lydian*)	136
A Pythian Ode, by Pindar (*Phrygian*)	93
A Sailor's Love-Song, of Leucadia (*Hypolydian*)	104
Alleluia of the Apostle, from Liturgy of the Russian Church (*Dorian*)	84
The Same, in Another Mode (*Mixolydian*)	106
Amén, from Coptic Liturgy of St. Basil (*Hypolydian and Hypodorian*)	100
An Adulatory Song, of Smyrna (*Pseudo-Hypomixolydian, A.*)	108
An Anxious-Lover's Song, of Athens (*Pure Chromatic*)	119
Coda to the Same (*Hypodorian*)	121
An Ardent-Lover's Song, of Smyrna (*Lydian; and Hyper Chromatic Lydian*)	133
An Exile's Song, of Smyrna (*Lydian*)	101
Aria Patetica, in Slow Dance measure (*Pseudo-Dorian B.*)	110
Benedictus, from Greek Liturgy of St. Basil (*Pure Chromatic; and Hypolydian, transposed*)	133
Boorlatskahyah, or Boatmen's Song, of Nizhni-Novgorod (*Hypodorian*)	89
Boorlatskahyah, or Boatmen's Song, of Tamboff (*Hypolydian*)	102
Chorovodnahyah, or Choral-Dance, of Astrakhan (*Hypolydian*)	103
Chorovodnahyah, or Choral-Dance, of Pramzeenah (*Hypophrygian*)	98
Chorovodnahyah, or Choral-Dance, of Semenoff (*Hypophrygian*)	82
Chorovodnahyah, or Choral-Dance, of Stavropol (*Hypophrygian*)	97
Transposed Version of the Same	100
The Same, in Another Mode (*Hypodorian*)	99
Chorus from the Oratoriette "Baptism" (*Dorian*)	84
Easter Hymn, from Service of the Greek Church (*Hypodorian*)	88
Gregorian Chant, Tone 1 (*Phrygian*)	13
Double Counterpoint Inversion of the Same (*Hypophrygian*)	18
Lancer's Quadrille: fragment of 1st figure (*Hypodorian, transposed; and Pseudo-Lydian, B.*)	110
Lesser Introit, from Sunday Liturgy of the Russian Church (*Dorian*)	83
The Same, in Another Mode (*Mixolydian*)	106
Melody of Fatma Sultana, Daughter of the late Sultan (*Hyper Chromatic Hypodorian; and Pure Chromatic*)	130
Melody of Geminiè Sultana, Daughter of the late Sultan (*Chromatic Lydian; and Hyper Chromatic Dorian*)	140
Melody of Rafiè Sultana, Daughter of the late Sultan (*Co-normal form of Hyper Chromatic Hypodorian; and Lydian*)	152
Metrical Psalm Tune, "Newtown" (*Lydian, transposed*)	19
Metrical Psalm Tune, "Old Hundredth" (*Hypolydian, transposed*)	19
Oriental Dance, from "Leblebidji Hor-hor Agha" (*Pure Chromatic*)	112
Osmaniè Imperial March (*Chromatic and Hyper Chromatic Hypodorian, transposed; Pure Chromatic, transposed; and Hyper Chromatic Hypodorian*)	136
Protiazhnahyah, or Continuous Song, of Pramzeenah (*Hypodorian*)	89
Song (without words) from "Leblebidji Hor-hor Agha" (*Chromatic Hypodorian*)	127
Svahdebnahyah, or Naptial Song, of Kniaghininski (*Hypophrygian*)	96
Svahdebno-Shootochnahyah, or Merry-Nuptial Song, of Niahogorod (*Phrygian*)	94
Trisagion, from Coptic Liturgy of St. Basil (*Hypophrygian*)	97
Triumphal Hymn, from Coptic Liturgy of St. Basil (*Dorian*)	83
Troparion, from Aposticha at Vespers, on Good Friday, in the Greek Church (*Chromatic Phrygian*)	135
Turkish Schiarky (*Pure Chromatic*)	112
Turkish Schiarky (*Pure Chromatic*)	114
Transposed Melody of the Same	118
Turkish Schiarky (*Pure Chromatic*)	116
Turkish Schiarky (*Pure Chromatic; and Hypodorian*)	122
Turkish Schiarky (*Pure Chromatic; and Hyper Chromatic Hypodorian*)	132

BYZANTINE MUSIC.

PART I.—PRELIMINARY.

IT is generally considered a sufficient answer, and an estoppel of all future enquiry, to inform those who wish to know something of the peculiarities of Eastern Music, sacred or profane, that not only is the system of tonality prevalent in the lands of the sun-rising widely divergent from that which now obtains in Europe, but also that it is impossible to represent the sounds of the Oriental scales by the modern Western notation.

2. There is a great deal of truth in this answer. Not only is the diatonic genus, although based on the same natural scale, very differently applied in the East to what it is in the West, but in addition there exists an entirely unknown ancient Oriental application of the chromatic genus, which, to most Western musicians, when thoroughly apprehended by them, appeals almost with the force of a new revelation.

3. So far, our ideal objector is perfectly right. The system of tonality in the East differs from that in the West. But when he urges the incapacity of our modern system of musical notation to represent the sounds of the Oriental scales, we may be pardoned for asking, previously to giving our assent or dissent, whether the words convey clearly the mind of the objector, or whether he does not assume in the distant unknown certain insoluble difficulties which notoriously beset his feet in the well-trodden paths nearer home? In other words, is it not less the incapacity of our modern system of notation with its thirtyone notes within the compass of an octave, than the folly of attempting with our artificial pianoforte division of the octave into twelve notes only, to represent the various tones of the Oriental chromatic genus, which lies at the root of our ideal friend's objection?

4. Every pianoforte student knows that there is a great difference of treatment and effect between c-sharp and d-flat, and between d-sharp and e-flat, but that he is obliged to make two black keys do duty for those two pairs of notes. In like manner the other three black keys do duty for six notes, two notes to each key. He knows also that each white key has to do duty for three notes, as, *e.g.*, c-doublesharp, d-natural, and e-doubleflat, which are produced by the white key known as D ; and so with each of the other six white keys.* This gives us ten notes from the five black keys, and twentyone notes from the seven white keys, a total of thirtyone notes within the compass of an octave : which thirtyone notes, we repeat, are represented on the pianoforte by twelve keys only. To the uninitiated observer it might seem as if the nineteen extra notes credited to the twelve pianoforte keys over and above their own proper sounds were purely imaginary. But the musical student is conscious of a still greater weakness than this. He knows that of the thirtyone notes in the octave, thirty, if not imaginary, are, so far as the pianoforte is concerned, the result of compromise, leaving one only, that whichever it be from which he starts his calculation, which can be assumed as perfect. If the pianoforte tuner, to make his small number of twelve notes in the octave at all accommodating to each other, has to resort to the division of a certain amount of surplus sharpness which remains after only twelve perfect fifths, which surplusage is styled "the wolf": how largely increased must not that surplusage or "wolf" be after thirtyone such perfect fifths have been calculated? This we will now endeavour to point out to the reader.

5. In the diatonic scale there are two varieties of each of the numeric intervals, minor and major. Thus, of the seconds there are two minor and five major ; of the thirds there are four minor and three major ; of the fourths there are six minor and one major ; of the fifths there are one minor and six major ; of the sixths and sevenths there are the converse of the thirds and seconds, as in the following :—

* See footnote to paragraph 318, in SUMMARY.

EXAMPLE I.

PRELIMINARY. 3

6. The one instance of the minor fifth (b-natural : f-natural) is dissonant, and does not at present concern us.

7. But the major fifth, of which there are six instances, is consonant, and not only so, but, being unvarying in its application to both "major and minor keys," is styled perfect; in this respect differing from the thirds and sixths, which, though consonant, are variable, and hence styled imperfect. Henceforth, in this work, the terms perfect and imperfect, consonant and dissonant, as applied to the major and minor fourths and fifths, being unnecessary, will be discontinued.

8. The two notes forming a major fifth are always represented by the proportional numbers 2 : 3,* the vibrations of the air necessary to produce that interval, whatever be their number, being always in that proportion. It will be a question of pleasant pastime for the reader to work out for himself a series of thirtyone such proportions, adding 50 per cent. each time to the number last recorded, thus, 2 : 3, 3 : 4·5, 4·5 : 6·75, &c.

9. If he does so, he will find by the time he has worked out the twelfth proportion that he is landed at 259·49267578125, whereas the distance he has traversed, seven octaves, presupposes only the plain number 256. It is this excess of 3·49267578125 over 256 that forms "the wolf" which perplexes others beside pianoforte tuners; and the reader will find, as he proceeds with his calculation, that the divergence sensibly increases.

10. But a shorter mode may be adopted for setting forth the difficulty, one which has the advantages over the former mode that it requires but six calculations per octave instead of twelve, and that it confines itself within the boundaries of its octave instead of wandering, like the former, over the whole compass of a modern seven octave pianoforte.

11. Three paragraphs back we mentioned that the proportion of the two notes forming a major fifth was as 2 : 3. The second such proportion in the proposed series was as 3 : 4·5. Let 2 stand for c-natural, then 3 will represent g-natural above, and 4·5 d-natural above that. D-natural is thus two major fifths, or an octave and a major second, above c-natural. Raise c-natural an octave to 4, so as to bring it into the close neighbourhood of d-natural, and c-natural : d-natural will stand as 4 : 4·5, or as 8 : 9. 8 : 9 is the accepted formula for the interval of a tone or major second.* A series of major seconds commencing with 8 : 9, and passing through two octaves, gives us the following curious results:—

B-sharp,	32·87912538286764174699783325195312 5
A-sharp,	29·22588922921568155288696289062 5
G-sharp,	25·9785682037427249145507812 5
F-sharp,	23·0920606255531311035156 25
E-natural,	20·526276111602783203125
D-natural,	18·245578765869140625
C-natural,	16·218292236328125
B-flat,	14·416259765625
A-flat,	12·814453125
G-flat,	11·390625
F-flat,	10·125
E-doubleflat,	9
D-doubleflat,	8 (To be read upwards from this root line.)

12. We here perceive that both of the pianoforte octave sounds, c-natural and b-sharp, while exceeding by the amount of their respective fractional decimal the plain double and quadruple of the d-doubleflat from which the series sprang, yet profess neither of them to have attained the octave limit, but bear in the nearer instance the title of augmented seventh, and in the remoter instance that of triply-augmented sixth. Thus the wider the intervals increase in actual distance, the narrower becomes their scale nomenclature. Curious anomaly this! And yet for those widening intervals with gradually contracting names the pianoforte, the modern musical be-all and end-all, has no sympathy, but forces all alike into its iron mould of twelve sounds only in the octave. That

* See paragraph 318, in SUMMARY.

B 2

instruments of the Violin family have greater freedom in this respect, giving the performer control over the notes produced, is no doubt one reason for the growing popularity of those instruments among ladies as well as gentlemen; and their influence, when once fairly established, will unquestionably and deservedly be permanent.

13. Yet improve or change our instruments as we may, the fundamental difficulty still remains unsolved, and we fear will ever so remain: how to proportion whatever intermediate intervals we have or may have so as to lead upward or downward to a true octave. We have seen how wide of the mark twelve major fifths land us. Six major seconds have answered our purpose no better, leaving us short of the octave though with extra vibrations. Three major thirds, whose proportion is 64 : 81,* when read upwards :—

    G-sharp, 102·515625 : B-sharp, 129·746337890625
    E-natural, 81   : G-sharp, 102·515625
    C-natural, 64   : E-natural, 81

produce exactly the same relative result as the upper of the two octaves in the previous table of major seconds; while four minor thirds, of the proportion 27 : 32,* also read upwards :—

    G-flat,   44$\frac{202}{729}$: B-doubleflat, 53$\frac{4577}{19683}$
    E-flat,   37$\frac{26}{27}$: G-flat,   44$\frac{202}{729}$
    C-natural, 32   : E-flat,   37$\frac{26}{27}$
    A-natural, 27   : C-natural, 32

produce the contrary effect of an increased nominal interval, the diminished ninth instead of the octave, with a reduced number of vibrations. Thus, while in the previous cases a nominal seventh gave us a sharpened octave, in this last case a nominal ninth makes compensation by giving us on its part a flattened octave. This is difficulty No. 1,—how to produce, by evolution from within its boundary limits, a true octave.

14. Difficulty No. 2 is of another kind. It is,—how, having possession of a true octave of which we are able to give no account, except that it is the result of a double number of atmospheric vibrations, to produce, by involution from its boundary limits, the place of any interval within the octave.† Until we can discover the central point of an

* See paragraph 318, in SUMMARY.

† We will here allude to one favourite way of adjusting the six intermediate diatonic notes which lie between the c-natural octave limits. We give the numbers in the normal diapason treated of presently in paragraph 17 :—

    C — 512 | F — 341⅓
    B — 480 | E — 320
    A — 432 | D — 288
    G — 384 | C — 256

Here we see the two tonal intervals, formed of the three lower notes in both these tetrachords, or groups of four notes, stand in the relation of 8 : 9 : 10, or 64 : 72 : 80, instead of in the proportional relationship, as at paragraph 17, of 8 : 9 : 10¼, or 64 : 72 : 81. This flattening of the major thirds, B and E, in the two tetrachords, paves the way for the flattening necessary to convert the augmented seventh into an octave: but at what a price is the convenience purchased! The sequence of major fifths (2 : 3) or their correlative inverted minor fourths (4 : 3), which had gone on smoothly from F to C,
        „ C to G,
        „ G to D, and
        „ D to A, is rudely broken, and the minor fourth, A : E, which should have stood as 4 : 3, or 108 : 81, is now extended to 108 : 80, and the lowered pitch is maintained in the remaining interval, E : B. So that there are really two distinct pitches, or planes of sound, introduced by this means into the natural diatonic scale, involving within the limits of an octave :—

Two kinds of major second—C : D, F : G, and G : A = 72 : 81, and D : E and A : B = 72 : 80 ;
Two kinds of minor third—D : F and A : C = 81 : 96, and E : G = 80 : 96 ;
Two kinds of major third—F : A = 64 : 81, and C : E and G : B = 64 : 80 ;
Two kinds of minor fourth—C : F, D : G, and G : C = 81 : 108, and E : A = 80 : 108 ;
A depressed major fourth—F : B = 56⅔ : 80, instead of 56⅔ : 81 ;
An extended minor sixth—E : C = 80 : 128, instead of 81 : 128 ;
Two kinds of major sixth—C : A = 48 : 81, and D : B = 48 : 80 ;
And a depressed major seventh—C : B = 42⅔ : 80, instead of 42⅔ : 81.

But all this mixing up of two kinds of the same interval affects only, as we have said, the seven notes of the diatonic scale, leaving the twentyfour remaining notes of the octaval thirtyone, to make their own terms with "the wolf," who is by no means satisfied with the concession thus far offered, irregular and make-shifty though it be.

octave which shall bear the same proportion to both its limits, we shall never be able to settle the places of the intermediate sounds except approximately. As the octave stands in the proportion of 1 : 2,* it is evident that with our present powers we shall never be able to work out a true solution. The same question under other forms—to ascertain the proportion of a diagonal to the sides of a square; or the proportion between the sides of two squares, the area of the one being double that of the other—has caused many a student's head to ache long previously to the musician even knowing his share of the difficulty, much less attempting to solve it.

15. Before saying our last word on this subject, we will allude to the second objection urged in the opening paragraph, and ask: Can the difficulty of representing the sounds of the Oriental scales by the modern Western notation be much greater than those we have been discussing, or can the failure be more conspicuous? We think we see our way to quite as fair an approximate result as has been thus far attained with Music which, because familiar, we consider better adapted to our means and requirements. Of course, the result we propose is only approximate, but that, we again assert, is all that any system of Music has thus far attained.

16. In the following *Table of Comparative Vibrations* of the thirtyone notes within the compass of an octave, the inequalities we have already pointed out are rendered palpable to all. We see, in illustration of difficulty No. 1, the great differences of effect in the two or three notes bracketed together under one pianoforte key, how that nominally lower notes, if sharp, are sharper than nominally higher notes on the same key; and *vice versa*, that nominally higher notes, if flat, are flatter than nominally lower notes. *E.g.*:—a-doublesharp, which comes immediately after the dividing line in the upper part of the *Table*, is appreciably sharper than b-natural or c-flat, though nominally lower than both; and c-flat is to the same extent flatter than b-natural or a-doublesharp, though nominally higher than both. In the same way with the black keys: a-sharp is sharper than b-flat, though nominally lower; and b-flat is flatter than a-sharp, though nominally higher.† We see also, in illustration of difficulty No. 2, how unequally the different internal notes are spread over the range of the octave limits. "The wolf" is here to be found in each note wherever we choose to search for it, proving the great necessity of the pianoforte tuner's empirical mean sound of the twelve keys which make up his octave.

17. We may mention, in conclusion of these preliminary remarks, that the following *Table of Comparative Vibrations*, specially calculated, has been based upon the old normal diapason of 512 vibrations per second in the open

* See paragraph 318, in SUMMARY.

† Some curious and instructive lessons may be learned by comparing the different numerals in the following *Table*. We will cite the case of the two pianoforte keys, 6 and 12, in which we find an apt illustration of the fact stated above in paragraph 12, that "the wider the intervals increase in actual distance, the narrower becomes their scale nomenclature." Thus, the above mentioned pianoforte keys, 6 and 12, furnish us

With one instance of the doubly-diminished sixth—
    e-sharp : c-flat, ... 1446·03922678272 : 2003·85994162176

With two instances of the minor fifth—
    e-sharp : b-natural, ... 1446·03922678272 : 2031·19913336832
    f-natural : c-flat, ... 1426·57607172096 : 2003·85994162176

With three instances of the major fourth—
    e-sharp : a-doublesharp, ... 1446·03922678272 : 2058·91132094049
    f-natural : b-natural, ... 1426·57607172096 : 2031·19913336832
    g-doubleflat : c-flat, ... 1407·37488355328 : 2003·85994162176

With two instances of the doubly-augmented third—
    f-natural : a-doublesharp, . . . 1426·57607172096 : 2058·91132094049
    g-doubleflat : b-natural, ... 1407·37488355328 : 2031·19913336832

And with one instance of the quadruply-augmented second—
    g-doubleflat : a-doublesharp, . . . 1407·37488355328 : 2058·91132094049

Here we see that the smaller nominal interval of the second (g-doubleflat : a-doublesharp) exceeds the vastly larger nominal interval of the sixth (e-sharp : c-flat) by 93·71572255417, although the pianoforte ignores the fact, and gives us the same sounds to represent not only those differing intervals, but the intermediate two thirds, three fourths, and two fifths also. We see, in addition, that the major fourths exceed the minor fifths, their supposed correlatives, by 27·71218757817 or 27·33019174656, according as they are calculated from e-sharp or f-natural.

tube of 12 inches, which gives to the natural notes of the diatonic scale the following numbers:—

$$\begin{array}{ll} C - 512 & F - 341\tfrac{1}{3} \\ B - 486 & E - 324 \\ A - 432 & D - 288 \\ G - 384 & C - 256 \end{array}$$

which numbers have been multiplied by 4·17942208512, the lowest common term comprehending all the thirtyone notes of the octave without a remainder. This, by the reduction of two octaves, is equivalent to raising the normal 512 to 534·96602689536, a numeral representing many a modern sharpened "concert pitch," so called.

18. TABLE OF COMPARATIVE VIBRATIONS
Of the Thirtyone Notes within the compass of an Octave.

Pianoforte Keys.	Notes.	Comparative Vibrations.	Order of Genesis.
1.	3. B-sharp,	2169·05884017408	(26)
	2. C-natural,	2139·86410758144	(14)
	1. D-doubleflat,	2111·06232532992	(2)
12.	31. A-doublesharp,	2058·91132094649	(31)
	30. B-natural,	2031·19913336832	(19)
	29. C-flat,	2003·85094162176	(7)
11.	28. A-sharp,	1928·05230237696	(24)
	27. B-flat,	1902·10142896128	(12)
10.	26. G-doublesharp,	1830·14339639688	(29)
	25. A-natural,	1805·51034077184	(17)
	24. B-doubleflat,	1781·20883699712	(5)
9.	23. G-sharp,	1713·82426877952	(22)
	22. A-flat,	1690·75082574336	(10)
8.	21. F-doublesharp,	1626·79413013056	(27)
	20. G-natural,	1604·89808068608	(15)
	19. A-doubleflat,	1583·29674399744	(3)
7.	18. F-sharp,	1523·39935002624	(20)
	17. G-flat,	1502·89495621632	(8)
6.	16. E-sharp,	1446·03922678272	(25)
	15. F-natural,	1426·57607172096	(13)
	14. G-doubleflat,	1407·37488355328	(1)
5.	13. D-doublesharp,	1372·60754729766	(30)
	12. E-natural,	1354·13275557888	(18)
	11. F-flat,	1335·90662774784	(6)
4.	10. D-sharp,	1285·36820158464	(23)
	9. E-flat,	1268·06761930752	(11)
3.	8. C-doublesharp,	1220·09550759792	(28)
	7. D-natural,	1203·67356051456	(16)
	6. E-doubleflat,	1187·47255799808	(4)
2.	5. C-sharp,	1142·54951251968	(21)
	4. D-flat,	1127·17121716224	(9)
1.	3. B-sharp,	1084·52942008704	(26)
	2. C-natural,	1069·93205379072	(14)
	1. D-doubleflat,	1055·53116260496	(2)

PRELIMINARY. 7

NOTE.—In the same connection as footnote † on page 5, we learn also by referring to the adjoining notes 13 and 14, and to the notes 31 and 1 separated by the line at head of the *Table*, how much nearer together are the quadruply-diminished fourths—d-doublesharp : g-doubleflat, and a-doublesharp : d-doubleflat—than are the minor seconds—c-natural : f-natural, and b-natural : c-natural—on the notes 12 : 15 and 30 : 2, represented by the same pianoforte keys 5 : 6 and 12 : 1. The two fourths are respectively distant 34·76733625562 and 52·15100438343, while the two seconds, nominally nearer though they seem, are respectively 72·44331614208 and 108·06497421312, or more than twice the distance of the two fourths. Yet fourths and seconds on the pianoforte are the same!

Another lesson we learn from the above *Table* is the great subdivision of which the ordinary musical degree or interval of the tone or major second is capable. Musical travellers in the East always tell us that the Oriental scale contains more notes than Western musicians are accustomed to. Some tell us positively that the tone consists of three parts instead of two, among whom Mr. Edward Lane, in his *Modern Egyptians* (London: Chas. Knight & Co., 1837), holds a distinguished place. His words, in vol. ii., page 64, are: "The most remarkable peculiarity in the Arab system of music is the division of tones into thirds." These words have been quoted again and again, and have probably, in many cases, prevented further enquiry on account of the seeming difficulty involved in them, and their contradiction of the pianoforte division of the tone into two parts only. The more scientific have attempted to meet the difficulty of the extra intervals by describing them as commas, or quarter-tones, and by the use of other explanatory terms which equally need explanation. But each and all of these writers understate the case. By tabulating the thirtyone notes within the compass of an octave we discover that while two of the notes are unable to make the step of a tone, of the twentynine notes which remain the tone in twentyone cases is divisible into five parts each, and in eight cases into six parts each, in ascending as well as in descending. Thus, if we take the b-natural of note 30 we find that the interval which separates it from a-natural of note 25, the tone below, is equal to, as a five part instance, ... 225·68879259648

of which b-natural	: c-flat	occupies	. . . .	27·33919174656
,,	o-flat	: a-sharp	,, ...	75·80763924480
,,	a-sharp	: b-flat	,, ...	25·95087341568
,,	b-flat	: g-doublesharp	,, ...	71·95803256440
,,	g-doublesharp	: a-natural	,, ...	24·63305362504
				225·68879259648

Or, if we take the b-flat, of note 27 we find that the interval which separates it from c-natural, of note 2 above the line at head of the *Table*, is equal to, as a six part instance in ascending, ... 237·76207862016

of which b-flat	: a-sharp	occupies	. . . .	25·95087341568
,,	a-sharp	: c-flat	,, ...	75·80763924480
,,	c-flat	: b-natural	,, ...	27·33919174656
,,	b-natural	: a-doublesharp	,, ...	27·71218757817
,,	a-doublesharp	: d-doubleflat	,, ...	52·15100438343
,,	d-doubleflat	: c-natural	,, ...	29·80178225152
				237·76207862016

Subjoined is a complete list of the twentynine possible tones in the descending and ascending series, with the number of intermediate degrees or intervals, 5 or 6, of which each tone is capable.

FIVEFOLD AND SIXFOLD DIVISION OF TONES.

	DESCENDING.			ASCENDING.	
31. A-doublesharp	to g-doublesharp,	5			
30. B-natural	,, a-natural,	5 ;	and to c-sharp,		6
29. C-flat	,, b-doubleflat,	5 ;	,, d-flat,		6
28. A-sharp	,, g-sharp,	5 ;	,, b-sharp,		6
27. B-flat	,, a-flat,	5 ;	,, c-natural,		6
26. G-doublesharp	,, f-doublesharp,	5 ;	,, a-doublesharp,		5
25. A-natural	,, g-natural,	5 ;	,, b-natural,		5
24. B-doubleflat	,, a-doubleflat,	5 ;	,, c-flat,		5
23. G-sharp	,, f-sharp,	5 ;	,, a-sharp,		5
22. A-flat	,, g-flat,	5 ;	,, b-flat,		5
21. F-doublesharp	,, e-sharp,	5 ;	,, g-doublesharp,		5
20. G-natural	,, f-natural,	5 ;	,, a-natural,		5
19. A-doubleflat	,, g-doubleflat,	5 ;	,, b-doubleflat,		5
18. F-sharp	,, e-natural,	6 ;	,, g-sharp,		5
17. G-flat	,, f-flat,	6 ;	,, a-flat,		5
16. E-sharp	,, d-sharp,	6 ;	,, f-doublesharp,		6
15. F-natural	,, e-flat,	6 ;	,, g-natural,		6
14. G-doubleflat	. . . .		,, a-doubleflat,		6

BYZANTINE MUSIC.

	DESCENDING.			ASCENDING.	
13. D-doublesharp	to c-doublesharp,	5			
12. E-natural	,, d-natural,	5;	and to	f-sharp,	6
11. F-flat	,, e-doubleflat,	5;	,,	g-flat,	6
10. D-sharp	,, c-sharp,	5;	,,	e-sharp,	6
9. E-flat	,, d-flat,	5;	,,	f-natural,	6
8. C-doublesharp	,, b-sharp,	5;	,,	d-doublesharp,	5
7. D-natural	,, c-natural,	5;	,,	c-natural,	5
6. E-doubleflat	,, d-doubleflat,	5;	,,	f-flat,	5
5. C-sharp	,, b-natural,	6;	,,	d-sharp,	5
4. D-flat	,, e-flat,	6;	,,	e-flat,	5
3. B-sharp	,, a-sharp,	6;	,,	c-doublesharp,	5
2. C-natural	,, b-flat,	6;	,,	d-natural,	5
1. D-doubleflat	.	.	,,	e-doubleflat,	5

If the reader thinks that the eleven places of decimals in the *Table of Comparative Vibrations* are somewhat of a burden, we assure him that it is the smallest numeral form he can resort to, and that it has the great advantage of presenting each note in the *same* numeral form. If he elects to start from unity for his thirtyone notes within the compass of an octave with the lowest generating note, g-doubleflat, though for a few calculations he save a little, he will find when he reaches the highest generated note of the species, a-doublesharp, that he is landed in fortyseven places of decimals, thus:—

ORDER OF GENESIS.	PROPORTIONAL VALUE.
(31) A-doublesharp,	1·46294448267276067099373004056847003489501933125
(30) D-doublesharp,	1·9505926435636908940583187207579612731933 10375
(29) G-doublesharp,	1·3003050057091205904388791471719741821 2890025
(28) C-doublesharp,	1·7338601276121007952518386629959655 76171875
(27) F-doublesharp,	1·1559067517414405301678925752639770 5078125
(26) B-sharp,	1·54120000232192070680052343388530 2734375
(25) E-sharp,	1·027472668214613804593682250123335 15625
(24) A-sharp,	1·36906355761945072791576385408046 875
(23) D-sharp,	1·82661607582398009705543518066 40025
(22) G-sharp,	1·21774538455065339803695578 7109375
(21) C-sharp,	1·623660512734204530715942382 8125
(20) F-sharp,	1·08244034182280302047729492 1875
(19) B-natural,	1·4432537890970706039697265 625
(18) E-natural,	1·924338385402760925292068 75
(17) A-natural,	1·282892256975173950195312 5
(16) D-natural,	1·71052300930023193350375
(15) G-natural,	1·14034867256682128900625
(14) C-natural,	1·52046489715576171875
(13) F-natural,	1·0136432647705078125
(12) B-flat,	1·35152435302734375
(11) E-flat,	1·802032470703125
(10) A-flat,	1·20135498046875
(9) D-flat,	1·001806640625
(8) G-flat,	1·06787109375
(7) C-flat,	1·423828125
(6) F-flat,	1·8984375
(5) B-doubleflat,	1·265625
(4) E-doubleflat,	1·6875
(3) A-doubleflat,	1·125
(2) D-doubleflat,	1·5
(1) G-doubleflat,	1

To be read upwards from the root line. Ascending major fifths to be calculated as 2 : 3; descending minor fourths 4 : 3.

PART II.—THE DIATONIC GENUS.

THE Music, sacred and profane, of the Eastern nations, Christian and non-Christian, within and adjoining the old Byzantine empire, is based primarily upon the chromatic genus containing two semitones in the tetrachord. The diatonic genus containing one semitone only in the tetrachord is also in use, but is seldom sustained exclusively for any length of time in practice, being blended, sooner or later, to a greater or lesser extent, with the chromatic genus. It is necessary, however, to consider first the diatonic genus.

20. Upon the nature of the tetrachord, and the position it occupies in the octave scale, depend the character of the Modo, or as it is commonly styled in Great Britain—"the Key." As we have already several times used the word *key* in a mechanical sense, applying it to the finger levers of the pianoforte, we prefer, rather than affix to the word a second sense, and write of "major keys," "minor keys," "keys of D, F," &c., to use either or both of the words *scale* and *mode*, which are equally widely accepted, and far more worthy of acceptance.

21. Of the diatonic tetrachord with one semitone only, there are three varieties · (1) that in which the semitone occupies the lowest interval; (2) that in which it occupies the central interval; and (3) that in which it occupies, as in most modern music, the highest interval, which is styled when so occupied the leading interval. These three varieties of tetrachord, whose differences of character are evident to all, have each two instances in the octave, forming the six minor fourths of Example I., as set forth in the following:—

EXAMPLE II.

where the second instance of each variety occurs in the second stave, immediately underneath its prototype.

22. An octave consists of two adjoined tetrachords. The three diatonic tetrachords with one semitone each of the above example, when interblended one with another, give nine distinct diatonic octave scales, of which five consist of natural notes only, and four have need of the transposing characters, sharps and flats. Of these four latter, two forms are given in their respective staves, in each of which one tetrachord is natural, the other transposed. The nine octave scales in the following example are set out differently in ascending and descending; the ascending scales lying between their more normal limits, those descending lying between the limits of a common octave—d-natural : d-natural. This latter arrangement shows more plainly to the unpractised eye the actual differences in the various scales.

EXAMPLE III.

23. Beside the three varieties of the diatonic tetrachord given above, there is still a fourth variety, differing essentially from its three companions. Those three, with their duplicates, each formed a minor fourth, and each contained within its limits two tones and one semitone. As we shall shortly see, much depends upon the relative position of those two tones and one semitone. But in this fourth tetrachord, forming the one major fourth of Example I., there is no semitonal interval. The three intervals are each in extent one tone: hence the common name of *triton* given to this major diatonic fourth. It is unmistakably dissonant.

EXAMPLE IV.

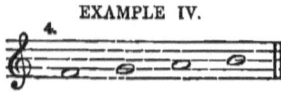

THE DIATONIC GENUS. 11

24. This tritonal tetrachord or major fourth, blended with the three tetrachords previously given, furnishes us with seven additional diatonic octave scales, of which seven two only consist entirely of natural notes. These two form respectively the most major of all the major scales (No. 12), with every intermediate interval major, as in bar 4 of Example I., read vertically; and the most minor of all the minor scales (No. 13), with every intermediate interval minor, as in bar 7 of Example I., read also vertically.* The remaining five are assisted by sharps and flats, and have, as in Example III., two instances in each stave. The descending scales have also the previous common octave limit.

EXAMPLE V.

25. The first remark we will make in reviewing the above sixteen diatonic octave scales, is, that excepting the last, No. 16, they obviously divide themselves into three classes or families: (1) that in which all the notes are natural, and deserves that all its scales be styled *Natural Diatonic*; (2) that in which one sharp or one flat is needed for its normal definition; and (3) that which has similar need for two sharps or two flats. The two latter, by their newly imported notes, earn for their respective scales the title of *Artificial Diatonic*, A and B.

* All other major scales contain one or more minor intervals, and the other minor scales contain one or more major intervals. See paragraphs 311 and 312, in SUMMARY.

26. Of the first class, all the seven possible tetrachords are made available in the formation of seven diatonic scales, thus:—

```
       No. 13.            No. 9.            No. 4.            No. 1.
    b c d e | f g a b | c d e f | g a b c | d e f g | a b c d | e f g a | b c d e
             No. 12.            No. 6.            No. 2.
```

27. Of the second class, five diatonic octave scales only are possible; two, those commencing with f-natural and c-sharp, being precluded on account of the tetrachord *c d e f*, which forms a diminished fourth belonging to the chromatic genus. Omitting the alternative scales in Examples III. and V. with one flat, we append those with one sharp, and designate the sharpened note by an *italic* letter.

```
       No. 14.                            No. 8.            No. 3.
    b c d e | f g a b | c d e f | g a b c | d e f g | a b c d | e f g a | b c d e
                                 No. 11.            No. 5.
```

28. Of the third class with two sharps or two flats, there are possible only three diatonic octave scales, those commencing with e-natural, a-natural, and b-natural. The scales commencing with f-natural and c-sharp are precluded by a second variety of the diminished fourth—*c d e f*; and those commencing with g-natural and d-sharp by yet a third variety of the diminished fourth—*d e f g*. These two latter varieties of the diminished fourth, as we shall presently see, though chromatic in the modern sense of the term, form no part of the Oriental chromatic genus.

```
       No. 15.                                              No. 7.
    b c d e | f g a b | c d e f | g a b c | d e f g | a b c d | e f g a | b c d e
                                                                No. 10.
```

29. The differences of character observable in these three classes of diatonic scale are traceable entirely to the relative disposing of the semitones in the two tetrachords. In the first or natural class the semitones occur after intervals of three and two tones alternately, thus:—

$$\begin{array}{cccccccccccc} 1 & 2 & 3 & & 1 & 2 & & 1 & 2 & 3 & & 1 & 2 \\ f & g & a & b\text{-}c & d & e\text{-}f & g & a & b\text{-}c & d & e\text{-}f, & \&c. \end{array}$$

in the second class they occur after intervals of four tones and one tone alternately, thus:—

$$\begin{array}{cccccccccc} 1 & 2 & 3 & 4 & 1 & 1 & 2 & 3 & 4 & 1 \\ f & g & a & b & c\text{-}d & e\text{-}f & g & a & b & c\text{-}d & e\text{-}f, & \&c., \end{array}$$

while in the third class the two semitones occupy adjoining positions after intervals of five tones, thus:—

$$\begin{array}{ccccccccccc} 1 & 2 & 3 & 4 & 5 & & 1 & 2 & 3 & 4 & 5 \\ f & g & a & b & c & d\text{-}e\text{-}f & g & a & b & c & d\text{-}e\text{-}f, & \&c. \end{array}$$

The greater and lesser dimensions of the tones and semitones we have endeavoured in this paragraph to illustrate by greater and lesser distances between the letters; and to show the gradually increasing groups of three, four, and five tones, have commenced each class of scale with f-natural, and distinguished the tonal distances by numerals. The group of three tones we have already, in paragraph 23, known as the *triton*; the groups of four and five tones were respectively known by the old Greeks as the *tetraton* and *pentaton*.

30. As a small mnemonic of these three classes of diatonic scale, it may be as well to point out: that while the three normal forms, Nos. 7, 8, and 9, commence in the sharp series with e-natural, d-natural, and c-natural; in the alternative series with flats each of the three alike commence with c-natural, thus:—

EXAMPLE VI.

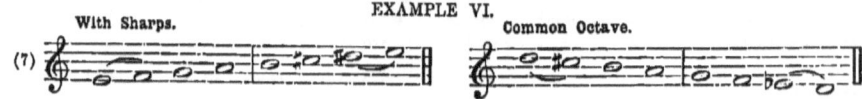

THE DIATONIC GENUS.   13

31. The octave from c-natural being covered by the *Table of Comparative Vibrations* at paragraph 18, we show the differences in the three classes of diatonic scales as represented by numerals contained in that *Table;* and we add in another column the lowest terms to which those numerals are reducible.

32. CLASS 1.—NATURAL DIATONIC SCALE.

NOTES.	COMPARATIVE VIBRATIONS.	LOWEST TERMS.
C-natural,	2139·86410758144	768
B-natural,	2031·19913336832	729
A-natural,	1805·51034077184	648
G-natural,	1604·89808068608	576
F-natural,	1426·57607172096	512
E-natural,	1354·13275557888	486
D-natural,	1203·67356051456	432
C-natural,	1069·93205379072	384

33. In the above column of *lowest terms* we have a set of numerals which represent a transposition of the scale into the normal pitch of g-natural, with f-sharp as the leading note on the second line.

34. CLASS 2.—ARTIFICIAL DIATONIC SCALE, A.

NOTES.	COMPARATIVE VIBRATIONS.	LOWEST TERMS.
C-natural,	2139·86410758144	691·2
B-natural,	2031·19913336832	656·1
A-natural,	1805·51034077184	583·2
G-natural,	1604·89808068608	518·4
F-natural,	1426·57607172096	460·8
E-flat,	1268·06761930752	409·6
D-natural,	1203·67356051456	388·8
C-natural,	1069·93205379072	345·6

35. In the above column of *lowest terms* we have a set of numerals which represent a transposition of the scale into a sharpened pitch of f-natural, with a-flat and b-flat instead of the e-flat and f-natural of the first column. The pitch, though sharp, is, nevertheless, not so sharp as that of the *Table of Comparative Vibrations*; c-natural, which is normal at 512, standing at 518·4 instead of 534·96602689536, as at paragraph 17.

36. CLASS 3.—ARTIFICIAL DIATONIC SCALE, B.

NOTES.	COMPARATIVE VIBRATIONS.	LOWEST TERMS.
C-natural,	2139·86410758144	622·08
B-natural,	2031·19913336832	590·49
A-natural,	1805·51034077184	524·88
G-natural,	1604·89808068608	466·56
F-natural,	1426·57607172096	414·72
E-flat,	1268·06761930752	368·64
D-flat,	1127·17121716224	327·68
C-natural,	1069·93205379072	311·04

37. In the above column of *lowest terms* we have a set of numerals which represent a flattened pitch of the co-normal scale of c-natural, with c-sharp and d-sharp instead of a-natural and b-natural. The flattening of the pitch is considerable: still, it does not reach to the semitone below, even of the sharpened pitch of the last previous scale of f-natural, its d-sharp standing at 590·49 as compared with 583·2 for the previous d-natural.

38. We will remark next upon the above sixteen diatonic octave scales, that they are supposed to vary in degrees of purity. And though this may seem to many a mere fancy, yet a little reflection will show that there is more in the supposition than is at first evident.

39. No one, for instance, will deny that the last scale on the list, No. 16, which we passed by in our previous remark, is thoroughly unworkable, and worthy of the place it occupies. The causes of its unworkableness are (1) that the two tritonal tetrachords of which it consists are incapable of junction, the initial note of the second tetrachord (f-natural or e-flat) being actually lower in pitch than the final note of the first tetrachord (c-sharp or b-natural); and (2) that it contains no semitonal interval, the chief ingredient of character.

40. The least perfect of the remaining fifteen scales which possess character are unquestionably those which admit one instance of the tritonal tetrachord of Example IV., and of these there are two varieties: (1) those which have the triton in the upper tetrachord; and (2) those which have the triton in the lower tetrachord. Those scales which have the triton in the upper tetrachord are not merely top-heavy in appearance, but are lacking in the major fifth; which lack has always been regarded as an imperfection, though little heeded as such in practice. With this least perfect class in its two varieties we will commence our list.

EXAMPLE VII.

1. SCALES HAVING THE TRITON IN THE UPPER TETRACHORD.
Common Octave.

THE DIATONIC GENUS.

2. Scales having the Triton in the Lower Tetrachord.

41. The scales formed from two of the tetrachords with a semitonal interval in Example II., increase gradually in importance from (1) that which has need of two sharps or two flats, to (2) those which have need of one sharp or one flat only; thence finally to (3) those which consist solely and simply of natural notes. We resume our list with the first two of these three classes.

EXAMPLE VIII.

3. Scale with Minor Fourth Tetrachords needing Two Sharps or Two Flats.

4. Scales with Minor Fourth Tetrachords needing One Sharp or One Flat.

42. Of the scales which consist solely and simply of natural notes, and have no need of sharp or flat, there are two varieties: (1) those in which the two tetrachords differ; and (2) most perfect of all, those in which the two tetrachords are of the same form. These varieties complete our list of gradually increasing degrees of purity.

EXAMPLE IX.

5. Natural Scales with Tetrachords Differing in Form.
Common Octave.

6. Natural Scales with Tetrachords Similar in Form.

43. Another property possessed by the above sixteen diatonic octavo scales, which calls for remark, is the capacity of each for treatment in Double Counterpoint. Even No. 16, unworkable in practice though it be, possesses this property in the most important numeric interval.

44. In the scales Nos. 4, 5, 7, and 16, the respective pairs of tetrachords are the exact converse of each other. This fact enables these four scales to adapt themselves naturally to the exigencies of Double Counterpoint in the *Octave*, thus :—

EXAMPLE X.

45. Double Counterpoint in the *Ninth* is formed in three instances by the junction of the scales Nos. 2, 3, and 15 with Nos. 6, 8, and 10, in contrary motion, thus :—

EXAMPLE XI.

46. Double Counterpoint in the *Tenth* is the product of the junction of scales Nos. 1 and 14 with Nos. 9 and 11 :—

EXAMPLE XII.

47. And lastly, one instance of Double Counterpoint in the *Eleventh* is furnished by the junction of the two remaining scales :—

EXAMPLE XIII.

Scales Nos. 13 and 12.

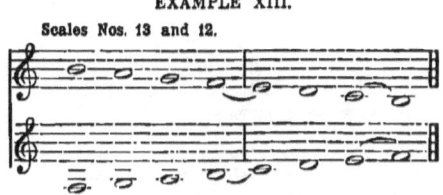

48. One advantage of this superior wealth (more than double that known to the West) of the Oriental diatonic genus, and its Double Contrapuntal facilities, is, that an Eastern musician has no temptation to take a melody based

upon one scale or mode, and treat it, on his own private judgment, as if based upon another scale or mode. He would never, for instance, think of taking the well-known Gregorian Chant of the 1st Tone, based upon scale No. 4 :—

EXAMPLE XIV.

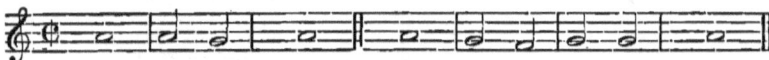

and treat it as if it were based upon scale No. 9 transposed from c-natural to f-natural, and commonly called f-major with one flat. Neither would he take its Double Counterpoint equivalent :—

EXAMPLE XV.

and treat it as if based upon the scale of g-major with one sharp. But he would hold both to belong to their normal scale, the natural scale of d, as in No. 4, the first as a dominant form, the second as a subdominant inversion, and attack them boldly in obedience to the laws of that scale, thus :—

EXAMPLE XVI.

"GREGORIAN TONE I.; FIRST ENDING."

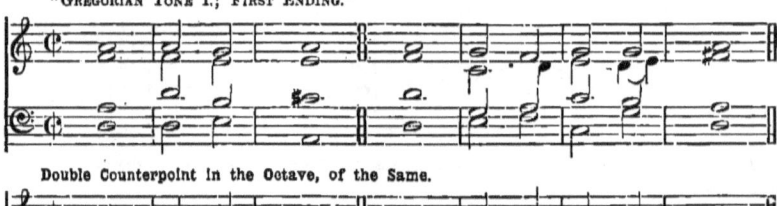

Double Counterpoint in the Octave, of the Same.

Double Counterpoint in the Eleventh, of Basso.*

49. But we are anticipating somewhat; and as a question of fact Eastern musicians do not know this particular Chant, though its parent scale is familiar enough to them. The evil protested against, that of injudicious admixture of Modes, must be held responsible for the digression.

50. In proceeding now to classify the above diatonic scales after the Oriental manner, we will, as a first

* It is noticeable that this Basso makes octaves and fifths to the melody in place of the fifths and octaves of the parent Chant.

step, ask the reader to compare attentively the two following, well-known, excellent Psalm tunes. The former of the two is better known in England by the name "London New," but we prefer to retain its older name "Newtown," which that learned musician, the late Rev. W. H. Havergal, in his Preface to *Old Church Psalmody*, 1847, now unfortunately no longer in print, tells us "was probably called from Newton, the appendage to 'the *auld toun o'* Ayr.'" * Mr. Havergal further asserts that "the Scotch lay fair claim to its composition." Of the latter tune nothing can be said to increase its fair fame; and since Mr. Havergal's *History of the Old Hundredth Psalm Tune with Specimens* (London: Sampson Low & Son, 1854), nothing further can be expected in elucidation of its origin.

EXAMPLE XVII.

"NEWTOWN." *From the* "Scotch Psalter," 1635. *Harmonised by* Rev. W. H. HAVERGAL.

"OLD HUNDREDTH." *From* "DAY'S Psalter," 1563. *Harmonised by* Rev. W. H. HAVERGAL.

---

* This mixing up of Newton and Newtown is Mr. Havergal's own, and it is now too late to get his explanation or correction. *The Penny Cyclopædia*, 1835, gives the name repeatedly in two words, as New Town (AYR).

51. These two tunes are here set in what most musicians would style the same "key of f-major." In general harmonic effect there is little or no difference between them. Both commence and finish upon the same tonic, which tonic is governed at the close by the same dominant harmony in the same quint position. It is true the greater number of notes of double length in the latter tune causes it to be a little more time-taking, and so to appear somewhat heavier; and this is a very fair description of the difference which distinguishes the latter tune from its more rapid and sprightly precursor. But the real cause of the respective sprightliness and heaviness of these two tunes is not in the mere difference of time consumed (the tunes stand respectively in note length as 3 to 4), but in a far more deep-seated fact, the fact that *the compass* of the two tunes is not the same. Both commence upon the same note, f-natural: yet while "Newtown" ascends to f-natural an octave higher, "Old Hundredth" ascends to the dominant, c-natural, only. But the three notes wanting to the upper compass of the latter tune are supplied downward, for whereas "Newtown" does not descend below its commencing note, "Old Hundredth" descends to the dominant on c-natural below. So that the compass of the two tunes is as exhibited in the following:—

EXAMPLE XVIII.

Tonic octave compass of "NEWTOWN." Scale No. 9 transposed.

Dominant octave compass of "OLD HUNDREDTH." Scale No. 6 transposed.

52. We ask the reader to notice particularly the difference in the two scales in this last example. Both are scales of the same tonal class, but the latter is evidently a development of the former. But a development in which direction, upward or downward? Ostensibly downward, as the latter descends three notes below the tonic, and would be styled by Western musicians a *hypo* or *plagal* of the former scale. But looking at the two scales as they stand in their tetrachordal relation, we see at once that, in spite of the lowered pitch of the latter (the notes where agreeing in name being an octave apart), and in spite also of the inferior position claimed for that latter by the title *hypo*, the development is clearly upward. The three bar measures each contain a tetrachord, and the growth is to the right hand in an upward direction, as follows: the flattened notes being represented by small capitals.

No. 9, transposed.

f g a B | c d e f | g a B c

No. 6, transposed.

53. This upward growth of its plagal scales it is which characterises the Gregorian development of the older musical system founded upon the scales Nos. 4, 1, 12, and 6, formulated by, and named after, the great St. Ambrose of Milan. A few words will serve to explain this Gregorian development, a clear appreciation of which is necessary for the true understanding of the Oriental application of the diatonic genus.

54. In previous paragraphs we pointed out the relative degrees of purity of the different scales, and proceeded to show their capacity each for Double Counterpoint. The sixth, or highest class of purity, the two tetrachords of each octave scale being similar, was claimed for Nos. 1, 4, and 9; the highest order of Double Counterpoint, that in the Octave, was the property of Nos. 4, 5, 7, and 16, the two tetrachords of each being converse. The one scale which combines both these merits is No. 4. No. 4 is the 1st Tone of both the Ambrosian and Gregorian systems of scales, and is styled *The Dorian Mode*.

THE DIATONIC GENUS.

EXAMPLE XIX.
Common Octave.

55. Scale No. 1, also of the sixth or highest degree of purity, yet unable to form, without the concurrence of No. 9, a Double Counterpoint, is the 2nd Tone Ambrosian and the 3rd Gregorian, and is styled *The Phrygian Mode*.

EXAMPLE XX.
Common Octave.

56. Scale No. 12, of the second degree of purity only, with dissimilar tetrachords, one of them being the tritonal dissonance, and with capacity, in concurrence with No. 13, for only the (as yet) most distant numeric order of Double Counterpoint, forms the 3rd Tone Ambrosian and the 5th Gregorian, and is styled *The Lydian Mode*.

EXAMPLE XXI.
Common Octave.

57. Scale No. 6, of the fifth degree of purity, with dissimilar tetrachords, but both possessing the semitonal interval, and with the capacity of concurring with No. 2 to produce the second order of Double Counterpoint, is the 4th Tone Ambrosian and the 7th Gregorian, and is styled *The Mixolydian Mode*.

EXAMPLE XXII.
Common Octave.

58. These four Ambrosian Tones are, in the Gregorian system, regarded as of primary importance, as, in fact the only "authentic" Modes. They did sole duty in the West, for it is impossible to say how long, previous to St. Ambrose's time * as well as after. An extension of each scale was, however, at last found necessary to regulate the growing mass of musical matter, which already in Pope Gregory's time, by its tendency to increased compass, had outrun the limits of the authentic or primary Modes, and the following plan of extension was adopted.

59. The four Ambrosian Modes are thus constituted, in alphabetical order :—

1. The Dorian Mode, ... d e f g | a b c d
2. The Phrygian Mode, ... e f g a | b c d e
3. The Lydian Mode, ... f g a b | c d e f
4. The Mixolydian Mode, ... g a b c | d e f g

* This is, of course, mere conjecture on the part of those who advocate it, as little or nothing is known of the music prevalent in the West before the time of St. Ambrose (A.D. 333-397). Another tradition, claiming an Antiochene origin for the Ambrosian tonal order of intermodal progress, is alluded to in the second footnote to paragraph 63.

22   BYZANTINE MUSIC.

and a very little consideration would be sufficient to show the reforming Pope Gregory or his advisers, that to take the second Dorian tetrachord, a b c d, and append to it the first Phrygian tetrachord, thus: a b c d | e f g a, is in effect to make a new scale, which is really, from a Western point of view, a Doriophrygian Mode. The same process applied to the second Phrygian and first Lydian tetrachords, would produce a Phrygiolydian Mode or scale: b c d e | f g a b; and so with the second Lydian and first Mixolydian tetrachords: c d e f | g a b c. But in naming these new scales, which, as we have seen, are each a portion of two adjoining scales, it pleased their projector or projectors to ignore altogether the source of their new upper tetrachord, and claim relationship with the scale only which furnishes the lower tetrachord. Hence it is that—

        The Doriophrygian, . . . a b c d | e f g a has become *The Hypodorian Mode.*
        The Phrygiolydian,   . . . b c d e | f g a b has become *The Hypophrygian Mode.*
        The Lydiomixolydian, . . . c d e f | g a b c has become *The Hypolydian Mode.*

60. The Modes of the Gregorian system formed thus of the four Ambrosian and the three composite scales just given, are regulated in the following order, the new Modes each following the parent whose name it bears:—

EXAMPLE XXIII.
GREGORIAN SERIES.
The Dorian Mode. 1st Tone.
Common Octave.

The Hypodorian Mode. 2nd Tone.

The Phrygian Mode. 3rd Tone.

The Hypophrygian Mode. 4th Tone.

The Lydian Mode. 5th Tone.

The Hypolydian Mode. 6th Tone.

The Mixolydian Mode. 7th Tone.

THE DIATONIC GENUS.

61. With the 8th and the so-called 9th Gregorian Modes we have here nothing to do, since they are, as scales, merely repetitions of Tones 1 and 2 And so of any further extension of the numbers; they can be obtained only by repetition of some of the foregoing.

62. The great point we wish to be borne in mind is, that the Western hypo or plagal Modes are a development to the right hand, in an upward direction.

63. *In the East the exact opposite is the case.* Even in the secular books of instruction authorised by the Ottoman Government for use in the Turkish Empire, the title of one of which is at the foot of this page,* though they agree with the Western order of Tones commencing with d-natural as the basis, and so proceed to e natural, f-natural, and g-natural, for the second, third, and fourth Tones, as in the Ambrosian reckoning, yet they never swerve from the ecclesiastical and ancient Greek manner of development, which is *to the left hand, in a downward direction.*†

64. In illustration of this we will take the Dorian Mode of the West which corresponds to Tὸ Διουγκιάχ of the secular Araboperṣoturkish system (τὴν Ἀραβοπερσοτουρκικήν), and compare the respective development of their hypo or plagal Modes.

65. The Dorian Mode forms its plagal upwards, thus:—

No. 4.
d e f g | a b c d | e f g a
No. 2.

Tὸ Διουγκιάχ forms its plagal downwards, thus:—

No. 4.
g a b c | d e f g | a b c d
No. 6.

66. We see from this example, that while the Dorian Mode took its upper tetrachord, and appended to it the tetrachord next above it in pitch, to produce its plagal. Tὸ Διουγκιάχ took its lower tetrachord, and prefixed to it the tetrachord next below it in pitch, and thereby produced its plagal, a genuine *hypo*, which is named Tὸ Γιεγκιάχ, and is the lowest scale of the Araboperṣoturkish system.

67. The same method of treatment is adopted with the other three primary modes, and the total result of the secular Oriental diatonic system of scales is as follows (to be read upwards):—

NAME.	NUMBER.	COMPASS.	GREGORIAN EQUIVALENT.	NUMBER.
Tὸ Νεβά,	4th Tone,	G to G,	The Mixolydian Mode,	7th Tone.
Tὸ Τζιαργκιάχ.	3rd Tone,	F to F,	The Lydian Mode,	5th Tone.
Tὸ Σεγκιάχ,	2nd Tone,	E to E,	The Phrygian Mode,	3rd Tone.
Tὸ Διουγκιάχ,	1st Tone,	D to D,	The Dorian Mode,	1st Tone.
Tὸ 'Ράστ,	4th Plagal,	C to C,	The Hypolydian Mode,	6th Tone.
Tὸ 'Αράκ,	3rd Plagal,	B to B,	The Hypophrygian Mode,	4th Tone.
Tὸ 'Ασηράν,	2nd Plagal,	A to A,	The Hypodorian Mode,	2nd Tone.
Tὸ Γιεγκιάχ,	1st Plagal,	G to G.		

*ʹ ΜΕΘΟΔΙΚΗ ΔΙΔΑΣΚΑΛΙΑ ΘΕΩΡΗΤΙΚΗ ΤΕ ΚΑΙ ΠΡΑΚΤΙΚΗ πρὸς ἐκμάθησιν καὶ διάδοσιν τοῦ γνησίου ἐξωτερικοῦ μέλους τῆς καθ' ἡμᾶς Ἑλληνικῆς Μουσικῆς κατ' ἀντιπαράθεσιν πρὸς τὴν Ἀραβοπερσικὴν Συναρμολογηθεῖσα ὑπὸ τοῦ μουσ Π. Γ. ΚΗΑΤΖΑΝΙΔΟΥ Προυσσαέως. Ἀδεία τοῦ Αὐτ Ὑπουργείου τῆς Δημοσίας Ἐκπαιδεύσεως ὑπʹ ἀριθ. 24. (2 Ζιλχιδξέ 98 14 Τισρίου Ἐββὶλ 97.) Ἐν Κωνσταντινουπόλει' Α. Κορομηλᾶ καὶ υἱοῦ 1881.

† This blending of the Ambrosian order of the authentic modes with the Greek manner of development of the plagal modes, now established, by Turkish imprimatur, as the official secular use, gives rise to some curious speculation. The plagal modes of both the Eastern and Western diatonic systems, being a comparatively modern conception as compared with the parent authentic modes, took respectively the downward and upward progression which the parent modes had previously taken. This is perfectly comprehensible, though the reason of the Western or Ambrosian progression first differing from the old classical Greek progression is not easy to say. But why, in the modern Turkish secular use as taught in schools, should the Ambrosian upward order of the authentic modes be blended with the Eastward downward development of the plagal modes? We think the true answer to this question is something as follows. Mr. Kiltzanides, of Broussa, the author of the present Method, impressed, as most Eastern scholars are, by the superior scientific attainments of the West, thought it wise to conciliate, as well as he could, the two lines of thought: and as St. Ambrose must have found somewhere in the East, probably in the restlessly intellectual Antioch, the modal order now bearing his name, which order some Russian writers affect to prefer, he felt he could plead for its use, if not great, yet sufficient antiquity, and still better, a large field of acceptance. Hence his upward order of intermodal progress. But the downward development of the plagal modes was so thoroughly Eastern, and so uncontested, that nothing could be done therewith but leave it exactly as it stood. Hence his modern blend of the two systems. He trusts, no doubt, for his new commixture, the chances of life which other hybrids possess.

BYZANTINE MUSIC.

68. But it is with the Oriental ecclesiastical arrangement of the Modes, the more ancient and the more classical,* that we concern ourselves at present; and generally, henceforth, unless mention is made to the contrary. And here not only does the same rule obtain which we have just illustrated in the Oriental secular school, of forming the plagal Modes by adding to the side (τὸ πλάγιος) in such a way as to produce a *hypo* never to be confounded with a *hyper*, in this respect alone marking a broad line of severance from the West; but we find in addition an entirely different set of primary or fundamental Modes with quite another order of intermodal progress.

69. The Western order of intermodal progress, as well as its plagal development, were both upward.

70. The Oriental secular order of intermodal progress was upward, but its plagal development was downward.

71. But the Oriental ecclesiastical and classical order of intermodal progress, as well as its plagal development, are both downward.

72. Thus, the Western (Gregorian) and Oriental secular Modes both read upward, as follows:—

7th Tone,	The Mixolydian Mode,	G to G,	Τὸ Νιβά,	4th Tone.
5th Tone,	The Lydian Mode,	F to F,	Τὸ Τζιαργκιάχ,	3rd Tone.
3rd Tone,	The Phrygian Mode,	E to E,	Τὸ Σεγκιάχ,	2nd Tone.
1st Tone,	The Dorian Mode,	D to D,	Τὸ Διουγκιάχ,	1st Tone.

73. While the Oriental ecclesiastical and classical Modes read downward, as follows:—

ORIENTAL ECCL. AND CLASSICAL MODES.		COMPASS.	GREGORIAN EQUIVALENT.	NUMBER
1st Tone,	The Dorian Mode,	E to E,	The Phrygian Mode,	3rd Tone.
2nd Tone,	The Phrygian Mode,	D to D,	The Dorian Mode,	1st Tone.
3rd Tone,	The Lydian Mode,	C to C,	The Hypolydian Mode,	6th Tone.
4th Tone,	The Mixolydian Mode,	B to B,	The Hypophrygian Mode,	4th Tone.
1st Plagal,	The Hypodorian Mode,	A to A,	The Hypodorian Mode,	2nd Tone.
2nd Plagal,	The Hypophrygian Mode,	G to G,	The Mixolydian Mode,	7th Tone.
3rd Plagal,	The Hypolydian Mode,	F to F,	The Lydian Mode,	5th Tone.
4th Plagal,	The Hypomixolydian Mode,	E to E.		

74. The Dorian and Phrygian Modes respectively are here found to take each other's place and exchange notes; so do the Lydian and Hypolydian Modes; so also do the Mixolydian and Hypophrygian Modes. The Hypodorian Mode remains the same in both systems, though the parent Dorians themselves vary; and the Oriental Hypomixolydian Mode is unrepresented in the Gregorian system. It may also be mentioned that whereas in the Gregorian system two only of the primary modes, D and E, have their two tetrachords similar, in the Oriental ecclesiastical and classical system three of those modes are thus perfect, viz.:—E, D, and C.

EXAMPLE XXIV.

ORIENTAL NATURAL DIATONIC SERIES.

The Dorian Mode. 1st Tone.
Common Octave.

The Phrygian Mode. 2nd Tone.

* See Praeger and Ouseley's edition of Naumann's *History of Music* (London: Cassell & Co.), pages 133 and 181; and Ducoudray's *Trente Mélodies populaires de Grèce et d'Orient* (Paris: H. Lemoine), page 16.

THE DIATONIC GENUS.   25

The Lydian Mode.   3rd Tone.
Common Octave.

The Mixolydian Mode.   4th Tone.

The Hypodorian Mode.   1st Plagal Tone.

The Hypophrygian Mode.   2nd Plagal Tone.

The Hypolydian Mode.   3rd Plagal Tone.*

75. This very material difference both in the Modes and their formation may be further made evident in the following examples, which mark the upward and downward intermodal progress and the development of the respective plagal Modes. The upper brackets in both cases denote the authentic, primary, or fundamental Modes; the lower brackets denote the plagal Modes.

THE GREGORIAN SYSTEM OF MODES.
(Read from left to right.)

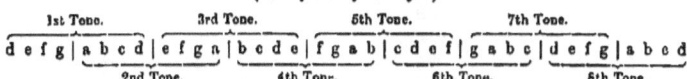

THE ORIENTAL ECCLESIASTICAL AND CLASSICAL SYSTEM OF MODES.
(Read from right to left.)

	4th Tone.		3rd Tone.		2nd Tone.		1st Tone.	
e f g a	b c d e	f g a b	c d e f	g a b c	d e f g	a b c d	e f g a	b c d e
	4th Plagal.		3rd Plagal.		2nd Plagal.		1st Plagal.	

* The Hypolydian Mode, 3rd Plagal Tone, is generally styled Βαρύς, or *Heavy* tone, hence the word Baritone. This word is now understood to mean a *Light* Basso part or voice.
The Hypomixolydian Mode, 4th Plagal Tone, has the same compass as the Dorian Mode, 1st Tone, and is here omitted.

E

76. The 8th Tone Gregorian and 4th Plagal Oriental, both named Hypomixolydian, develop each no new feature as scales, being in the one case higher, in the other case lower octave repetitions of their respective 1st or Dorian Tones.

77. Thus far the diatonic genus of the East has corresponded in the matter of notes with the diatonic genus of the West. The manner of forming the scales of each has differed, so also have the names of the scales themselves; but the individual notes have been the same. They all have been natural notes, and the scales formed by their means have all been natural, and constitute *The Oriental Natural Diatonic Series*. The 3rd Tone Oriental and 6th Tone Gregorian are very familiar to modern ears as the Major mode; while the 1st Plagal Oriental and 2nd Tone Gregorian have been generally regarded as the correct form of the Minor Mode, at least in descending.

78. Here it may be proper to observe that a favourite question with examiners of music in the present day is,—"How many Minor scales are there?" Whatever numerical reply they may expect, the question is evidently aimed at discovering whether or not the student is acquainted with a certain scale of the chromatic genus (No. 44), at which we shall presently arrive. But were the question restricted to the diatonic genus with minor and major tetrachords only, and to refer to all octave scales with a minor third, the student, with the information thus far given, might reply boldly,—"Eight, viz., Nos. 1, 2, 3, 4, 7, 8, 13, and 14." Reciprocally, in the same connection, there are also eight scales with major thirds, viz., Nos. 5, 6, 9, 10, 11, 12, 15, and the unworkable No. 16.

79. The aggregate of the degrees of purity in the primary and plagal ranks of both the Oriental and Gregorian systems undergoes no change. Although as primaries scales Nos. 13 and 9 take the place in the Oriental system of Nos. 12 and 6 in the Gregorian, the loss on No. 13 as compared with No. 12 is fully compensated by the gain on No 9 as compared with No. 6. No. 12 was already of low rank, the lowest but one, No. 13 is simply that one degree lower. No 6 was of the fifth class, No. 9 is of the sixth or highest class. The Double Counterpoint facilities also have undergone no change of any worth, for the inversion of No. 9 with No. 1, though of the *Tenth*, is quite as perfect, and more agreeable, than that of the *Ninth* with Nos. 6 and 2. Nos. 13 and 12 were already in concurrence.

80. We now approach the other two classes of scales in the diatonic genus of the East; those classes in which the tonal and semitonal intervals are differently grouped, which therefore have need, in their most normal form, of one and two sharps, or of one and two flats, and which constitute *The Oriental Artificial Diatonic Series*, A and B.

81. Let us briefly recapitulate what was said a few pages back, at paragraphs 25 and 29, respecting the *three* classes of diatonic scales. (1) When the two semitones per octave occur after intervals of three and two tones alternately, no sharp or flat is needed, excepting for transposing purposes. (2) When the two semitones occur after intervals of four tones and one tone alternately, one sharp or one flat is needed for its normal definition; and (3) when the two semitones occupy adjoining positions after intervals of five tones, two sharps or two flats are normally needed.

82. The second class of scales, that which has need in its most normal form of one sharp or one flat, is formed of Nos. 3, 5, 8, 11, and 14, and is styled *The Oriental Artificial Diatonic Series*, A. These scales are developed in the following order from right to left, commencing with No. 3. No. 14 is however in an anomalous position, having no parent from which to develop downwards, in consequence of f-natural being an impossible scale in this class, as before explained. It therefore takes the place of a Gregorian hypo by developing upwards from No. 3, but with the more appropriate title of a *hyper*. We select for illustration, as we did previously, the series needing one sharp.

$$\underbrace{g\ a\ b\ c}_{\text{No. 11.}}\ \Big|\ \underbrace{d\ e\ f\ g}_{}\ \Big|\ \underbrace{a\ b\ c\ d}_{\text{No. 8.}}\ \Big|\ \underbrace{e\ f\ g\ a}_{\text{No. 5.}}\ \Big|\ \underbrace{b\ c\ d\ e}_{}\ \Big|\ \underbrace{f\ g\ a\ b}_{\text{No. 14.}}$$

83. These scales being entirely of a composite nature, even in the upper or primary rank, have of necessity composite names to distinguish them, formed of the two tetrachords of the primary scales in the descending order, as follows :—

THE DIATONIC GENUS. 27

EXAMPLE XXV.
ORIENTAL ARTIFICIAL DIATONIC SERIES. A.
The Phrygiodorian Mode.
Common Octave.

The Lydiophrygian Mode.

The Hyperphrygiodorian Mode.

The Hypophrygiodorian, Doriolydian, or Hyperlydiophrygian Mode.

The Hypolydiophrygian Mode.

84. These scales also, it will be remembered, are of different degrees of purity: No. 14 being in the first or lowest class, and No. 11 in the class next above, both possessing the tritonal tetrachord, while Nos. 3, 8, and 5 are in the fourth class, and possess each two semitonal tetrachords.

85. The Double Counterpoint facilities, also, of these scales are very great No. 5 possessing within itself power for the *Octave* inversion, Nos. 3 and 8 possessing concurrent power to form the *Ninth;* and Nos. 14 and 11 concurring to form the *Tenth.*

86. One scale, moreover, of this second class, No. 8, was, until the last few years, the accepted ascending form of the Minor Mode in all English books of musical instruction.

87. The third class of Oriental diatonic scales, that which has need in its most normal form of two sharps or two flats, is formed, by three instances only, of Nos. 7, 10, and 15, and is styled *The Oriental Artificial Diatonic Series,* B. These scales are developed from right to left in the case of Nos. 7 and 10; No. 15 develops Gregorian fashion, and thus becomes a *hyper,* as did No. 14 in the second class of scales, and for exactly the same reason. We select for illustration the series needing two sharps.

No. 7.
a b c d | e f g a | b ♯ d e | f g a b
No. 10.   No. 15.

E 2

28   BYZANTINE MUSIC.

88. No. 7 being composed of a Lydian and Dorian tetrachord from right to left in the descending order, of necessity takes the compound name furnished by those tetrachords, and imparts the same to its dependant plagal Modes :—

EXAMPLE XXVI.
ORIENTAL ARTIFICIAL DIATONIC SERIES. B.
The Lydiodorian Mode.
Common Octave.

The Hyperlydiodorian Mode.

The Hypolydiodorian Mode.

89. No. 15 stands at the bottom of the lowest class of purity, and No. 10 stands last in the class above, both possessing the tritonal tetrachord; while No. 7, which possesses two semitonal tetrachords, has the honour of a third class entirely to itself. No. 7 also possesses the highest Double Counterpoint capacity, that of the introspective *Octave*, of which capacity the two previous classes of scales furnish only one instance each; and Nos. 15 and 10 concur to form a Double Counterpoint in the *Ninth*. The scale No. 7 is now more widely known in modern practice than it was. The first figure of the original *Lancers' Quadrille* affords a notable instance thereof, where the d-minor passage has an e-flat just before its close. Sir F. A. Gore Ouseley, Bart., the late Professor of Music in the University of Oxford, devotes pages 163-4 of his *Treatise on Harmony* (Oxford : Clarendon Press, 1868) to its discussion, and singularly enough, failing to trace the scale to its Eastern original, considers the second note of its lower Dorian tetrachord to be a "new" note. Three times is this epithet "new" applied to it, but it is highly appreciated notwithstanding, for it is also styled "pathetic," and "remarkable and very beautiful." So that our third class of Oriental diatonic scales, feeble though it be in numbers, and comparatively low as it certainly is in purity through the five tones in the octave standing together in one group, and forcing the two semitones into each other's arms, is evidently not lacking in dignity, being deemed worthy of homage by one who was perfectly competent to appraise the merits even of an unknown musical object.

90 The paucity of instances in this, the third class of Oriental diatonic scales, reminds us of the four exceptions already alluded to in paragraph 28 : "The scales commencing with f-natural and c-sharp are precluded by a second variety of the diminished fourth—*c d e f*; and those commencing with g-natural and d-sharp by yet a third variety of the diminished fourth—*d e f g*. These two latter varieties of the diminished fourth, . . . though chromatic in the modern sense of the term, form no part of the Oriental chromatic genus." The major fourth of Example IV. was formed by three intervals of one tone each; the three minor fourths of Example II. contained each two tones and one semitone; the two diminished fourths at present under consideration contain each one tone and two semitones, which tone and semitones are placed in inverse order in the two instances, making a small Double Counterpoint in the *Eleventh*, thus :—

c—d-e-f
g—f-e-d

91. It might be as well to remark, before bidding adieu to the diatonic genus and entering on a new phase of the subject, that all semitones thus far alluded to have been diatonic, as b-natural : c-natural, d-natural : c-sharp, &c., involving two different alphabetical names in each semitone. These, although minor seconds, are *major semitones*. We shall shortly have to make acquaintance with another kind of semitone, one which keeps the same alphabetical name, but alters its character : as d-natural : d-sharp, e-natural : e-flat, &c. These intervals of one alphabetical name, and styled augmented primes, are *minor semitones*.* Thus, a certain excepted interval which will shortly appear in this connection, a doubly-augmented second—c-flat : f-doublesharp, or d-flat : e-sharp—which the pianoforte assimilates not only to the major third, but also to the diminished fourth—d-sharp : g-natural, or c-sharp : f-natural—consists of one major semitone and three minor semitones, or of one tone and two minor semitones, thus, read upwards :—

F-sharp	: F-doublesharp.		*or,*
F-natural	: F-sharp.	E-natural	: E-sharp.
E-natural	: F-natural.	D-natural	: E-natural.
E-flat	: E-natural.	D-flat	: D-natural.†

The present diminished fourth tetrachords—*d e f g* and *c d e f*—on the other hand, consist of one tone and two major semitones, thus, also read upwards :—

F-natural	: G-natural.	E-natural	: F-natural.
E-natural	: F-natural.	D-sharp	: E-natural.
D-sharp	: E-natural.	C-sharp	: D-sharp.

These two instances of the diminished fourth tetrachord, connected as they are with the third class of diatonic scales, are clearly of diatonic development, and take their place, of right, equally with the dissonant major fourth of Example IV. in the diatonic series. They form a fifth and sixth variety of the diatonic tetrachord, as follows :—

EXAMPLE XXVII.

92. These two new tetrachords, blended with the four previously given, furnish us with twenty additional scales: the four scales—Nos. 20, 24, 29, and 34—omitted from the third class of Example XXVI., formed each by the junction of the diminished and tritonal tetrachords, which scales are allied directly to the diatonic genus; and sixteen others. Of these sixteen others, twelve, by their peculiar junction of the tetrachords in the octave, claim affinity with the chromatic genus. The whole of the twenty scales thus occupy, it will be seen, a kind of border-land, some inclining to the diatonic genus, others to the chromatic. As in Examples III. and V., we give one scale with sharps and one with flats, excepting only No. 35, which is too extreme to furnish either alone; and one instance, at the least, of each tetrachord in its normal form.

EXAMPLE XXVIII.

* See paragraphs 313 to 315, in SUMMARY. † See paragraphs 316 and 317, in SUMMARY.

THE DIATONIC GENUS. 31

93. Of the twelve scales which claim affinity to the chromatic genus, we will remark, though again somewhat anticipatively, that eight belong to eight distinct classes or families of scales in that genus, while four are monads. Nos. 23 and 26 represent two classes of seven members each ; Nos. 17, 21, 22, 27, 28, and 33 represent six classes of three members each ; and Nos. 18, 19, 31, and 32, which refuse to be classified, go to reinforce their five brethren of like unsocial nature, Nos. 42, 47, 55, 77, and 80, in the chromatic genus.

94. In like manner that we excepted No. 16 in Example V as unworkable, on the ground of redundance, so must we except Nos. 25, 30, 35, and 36 on the ground of deficiency: the two tetrachords in each scale being separated by a doubly-augmented second, an impossible interval (treated of above) of one major semitone and three minor semitones, or of one tone and two minor semitones.

95. Like No. 16 also, Nos. 30 and 35, though unworkable, have each the form capable of producing Double Counterpoint in the *Octave*, thus:—

EXAMPLE XXIX.

96. The twelve scales, which, by their peculiar junction of the tetrachords in the octave, claim affinity with the chromatic genus, are, by that same "peculiar junction," prevented from taking part in the ordinary production of Double Counterpoint, it being impossible to resolve any two of those scales into a common sequence of notes with

reversible intervals. But by taking heed to intervals only instead of notes, it is possible to evolve an illegitimate species of Double Counterpoint in the *Octave*, which, for practical purposes in this style of music, is not only admissible, but desirable. If we select the examples from the "Common Octave" series, the connection in the intervals, as well as the unlikeness of the notes, will be more readily traced. To these twelve semi-chromatic scales we add Nos. 25 and 36, the two unworkable scales which were not equal to the dignity of taking place with their fellows in Example XXIX.

EXAMPLE XXX.

97. Double Counterpoint in the *Eleventh* is formed, in one instance, by the junction of the scales Nos. 29 and 24;
98. And lastly, one instance of Double Counterpoint in the *Thirteenth* is furnished by Nos. 20 and 34.

EXAMPLE XXXI.   EXAMPLE XXXII.
Scales Nos. 29 and 24.   Scales Nos. 20 and 34.

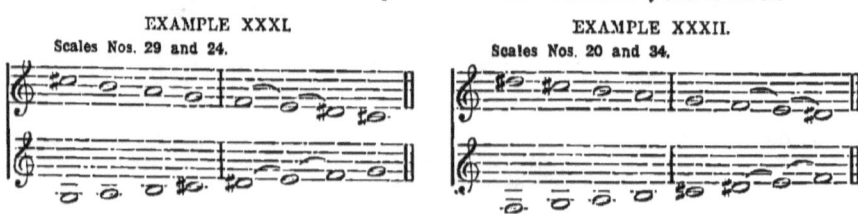

PART III.—THE CHROMATIC GENUS.

THE immense shadow of the Oriental Chromatic genus, bearing in its hand the grand total of twohundred and fiftythree * untransposed octave scales, each differing from all the others, now looms in sight, and familiar as we are with its appearance, we confess to considerable trepidation at its near approach, and almost shrink from the tentative task of opening up a few of its secrets, knowing well how much must of necessity be left unsaid on this great subject. No ingenuity has yet traced the intricacy of its varied ramifications, nor has the mystery of its vast depths yet been fathomed. We ask our readers to consider for a moment what is included under the term of "twohundred and fiftythree untransposed octave scales." The sixteen diatonic octave scales in Examples III. and V. are there presented, in the ascending and descending orders, *one*, No. 4, with one initial note (=1); *eight*, Nos. 1, 2, 3, 6, 8, 9, 12, and 13, with two initial notes (1+16=17); and *seven*, Nos. 5, 7, 10, 11, 14, 15, and 16, with three initial notes, each (17+21=38). Had the thirtyone notes within the compass of an octave been utilized as far as they could serve as initial notes, we should have had, instead of thirtyeight forms of those sixteen diatonic scales, no fewer than threehundred and seventytwo. If threehundred and seventytwo forms result from the transposition of sixteen scales only, what a proportionately larger number may be looked for from transposition of the twohundred and fiftythree additional chromatic scales! †

100. The chromatic genus of the East is based upon the following primary minor fourth tetrachord, of which there are two instances in both the sharp and flat series':—

EXAMPLE XXXIII.

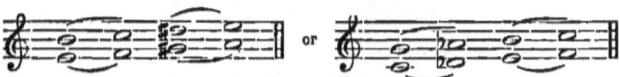

the two instances of which in both series' joined together form the parent octave scale, requiring two sharps or two flats for its normal definition, and whose four pairs of notes form each of them a major semitone :—

EXAMPLE XXXIV.

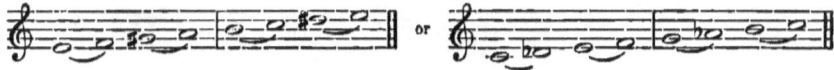

101. In like manner that we gave at paragraphs 32, 34, and 36, the parent scale in each of the three classes of the diatonic genus in the c-natural form, as contained in the *Table of Comparative Vibrations*, we now give the parent chromatic scale in the same pitch: in which pitch it also, like the two artificial classes in the above, requires flats for its normal definition.

---

* In the original article in *The Scottish Review* we used here the more modest, though sufficiently astounding, number "onehundred and eight." As we had not space to analyse the chromatic scales with the fulness with which we had treated the thirtysix diatonic scales, we therein confined ourselves to the result of the first twelve tetrachords only; and made no mention of the weeding out of certain undesirable though practicable families in that group, and of filling the vacant gaps in the more desirable families of scales by having recourse to the compound genus developed by the junction of the diatonic and chromatic tetrachords.

† See paragraphs 320 to 323, in SUMMARY.

102. THE CHROMATIC SCALE.

NOTES.	COMPARATIVE VIBRATIONS.	LOWEST TERMS.
C-natural,	2139·86410758144	622·08
B-natural,	2031·19913336832	590·49
A-flat,	1690·75682574336	491·52
G-natural,	1604·89808068608	466·56
F-natural,	1426·57607172096	414·72
E-natural,	1354·13275557888	393·66
D-flat,	1127·17121716224	327·68
C-natural,	1069·93205379072	311·04

103. In the above column of *lowest terms* we have a set of numerals which represent a flattened pitch of the co-normal scale of c-natural, with g-sharp and d-sharp. The flattening of the pitch, like that in paragraph 36, is considerable, and shows itself plainly in the c-natural on the third line, which stands at 491·52 instead of 512, as in paragraph 17. Still, it does not reach quite down to the level of b-natural, which is represented by 486.

104. It will be seen that the primary minor fourth chromatic tetrachord contains two semitonal intervals, and one augmented second, an interval of one tone and a minor semitone. The augmented second it is which gives to all Oriental music its peculiar character, and the position of that augmented second in the tetrachord has as great an influence as the position of the semitonal interval in the three diatonic tetrachords of Example II. It was the augmented second separating the two diatonic tetrachords of twelve scales in Example XXVIII. which gave to those scales the chromatic affinity to which we alluded. Two other forms of the minor fourth tetrachord are developed by the chromatic genus, as also two major fourth tetrachords, and one diminished fourth tetrachord, in manner following, taking as usual the series with sharps for our illustration, and reading from right to left:—

$$f\ g\ a\ b\ \underbrace{|\ c\ d\ e\ f\ |}_{\text{Major.}}\ \overbrace{\underbrace{g\ a\ b\ c}_{\text{ished.}}}^{\text{Minor.}}\ \underbrace{|\ d\ e\ f\ g\ |}_{\text{Dimin-}}\overbrace{a\ b\ c\ d}^{\text{Minor.}}\ \underbrace{|\ e\ f\ g\ a\ |}_{\text{Major.}}\overbrace{b\ c\ d\ e}^{\text{Minor.}}$$

105. We give in the following example the three minor fourth chromatic tetrachords in the order of their development: No. 7, the primary form, with four instances, having the augmented second in the central interval; Nos. 8 and 9, with each two instances, having the augmented second respectively, the one in the highest, the other in the lowest interval.

EXAMPLE XXXV.

106. These three minor fourth chromatic tetrachords, blended with the six tetrachords of the diatonic genus, furnish us with fortyfive new octave scales, the first instalment of the twohundred and fiftythree chromatic scales. We purposely avoid omitting any scale, that the reader may be furnished with all the tonal material available in the rich Oriental musical treasury. As in Example XXVIII. and previously, so here (excepting in Nos. 55, 77, and 80), and henceforth in the enumeration, we give one scale with sharps and one with flats; and one instance, at the least, of each tetrachord in its normal form.

THE CHROMATIC GENUS.

EXAMPLE XXXVI.

THE CHROMATIC GENUS. 37

107. The whole of these fortyfive scales are workable, without any exception. No. 44 is regarded by many in the present day as the ideal Minor Mode,* both in ascending and descending; and a hardy lecturer of some years since, in the writer's hearing, attributed its invention to Mendelssohn! This erroneous idea has perhaps been entertained by others.

* See observation at paragraph 78.

108. Nos. 49, 72, and 80 are capable each of producing Double Counterpoint in the *Octave*, thus :—

EXAMPLE XXXVII.

(1) Scale No. 49.

(2) Scale No. 72.   (3) Scale No. 80.

109. Forty of these scales, it being impossible to resolve any two of them into a common sequence of notes with reversible intervals, are susceptible only of the illegitimate kind of Double Counterpoint in the *Octave* of Example XXX., which is here also both admissible and desirable.

EXAMPLE XXXVIII.

(1) Scales Nos. 37 and 45.   (2) Scales Nos. 38 and 44.

(3) Scales Nos. 40 and 46.   (4) Scales Nos. 43 and 39.

(5) Scales Nos. 47 and 42.   (6) Scales Nos. 48 and 41.

BYZANTINE MUSIC.

THE CHROMATIC GENUS.

(19) Scales Nos. 64 and 81.   (20) Scales Nos. 77 and 55.

110. Nos. 54 and 78, the two remaining scales, concur to form a Double Counterpoint in the *Ninth*, thus:—

EXAMPLE XXXIX.

Scales Nos. 54 and 78.

111. Two major fourths are developed by the Chromatic genus against one in the Diatonic. Like that one, they are unmistakably dissonant in their external form, beside being chromatic in their internal incidence, the augmented second being respectively, the one in the highest, the other in the lowest interval. They here follow:—

EXAMPLE XL.

10.   11.

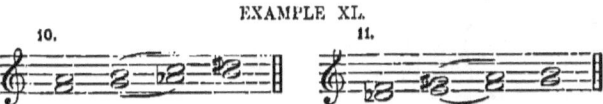

112. The forty new octave scales induced by these two major fourth chromatic tetrachords and their blending with the nine tetrachords already treated of, now follow. Nos. 99, 108, and 110 form exceptions to the rule of separate sharps and flats in each scale.

EXAMPLE XLI.

THE CHROMATIC GENUS.

43

THE CHROMATIC GENUS. 45

113. Of these forty scales, eight, Nos. 85, 94, 100, 104, 110, 114, 120, and 121, being composed of two major fourth tetrachords, are, like No. 16 in Example V., unworkable, and for the reasons there given. But like No. 16, two of the excepted scales, Nos. 110 and 120, are each invertible by Double Counterpoint in the *Octave*, thus:—

EXAMPLE XLII.

(1) Scale No. 110.   (2) Scale No. 120.

114. Thirtyfour of these scales, like the fourteen of Example XXX., and the forty of Example XXXVIII., form a portion of the series capable only of producing the illegitimate kind of Double Counterpoint in the *Octave*, thus:—

EXAMPLE XLIII.

(1) Scales Nos. 82 and 113.   (2) Scales Nos. 85 and 114.

(3) Scales Nos. 89 and 119.   (4) Scales Nos. 91 and 103.

(5) Scales Nos. 92 and 102.   (6) Scales Nos. 93 and 101.

(7) Scales Nos. 94 and 104.   (8) Scales Nos. 95 and 106.

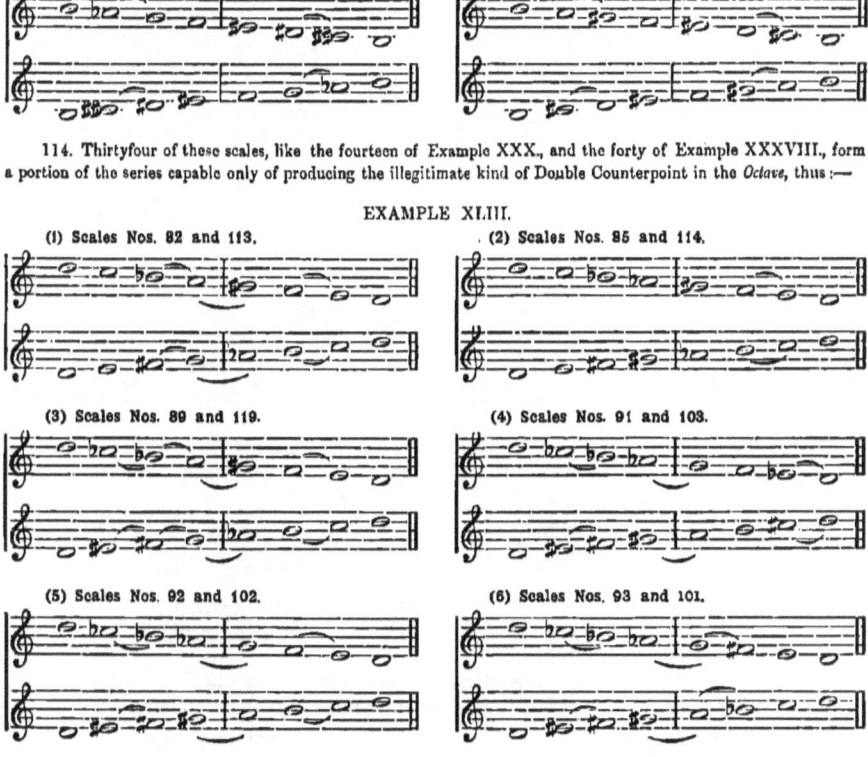

46   BYZANTINE MUSIC.

(9) Scales Nos. 96 and 105.

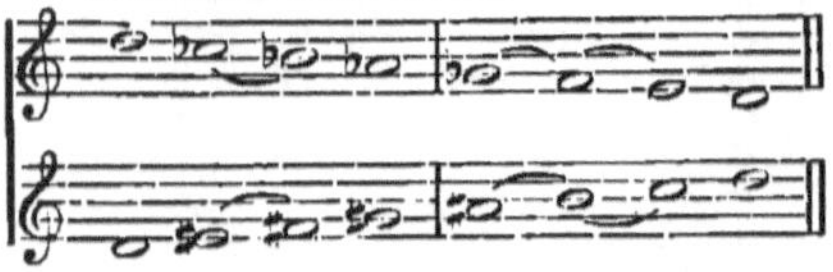

(10) Scales Nos. 97 and 107.

(11) Scales Nos. 99 and 108.

(12) Scales Nos. 100 and 121.

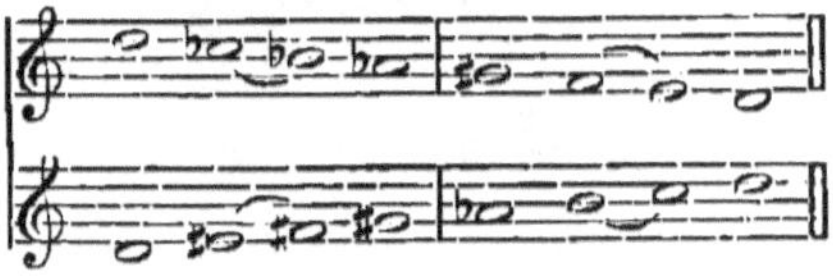

(13) Scales Nos. 111 and 84.

(14) Scales Nos. 112 and 83.

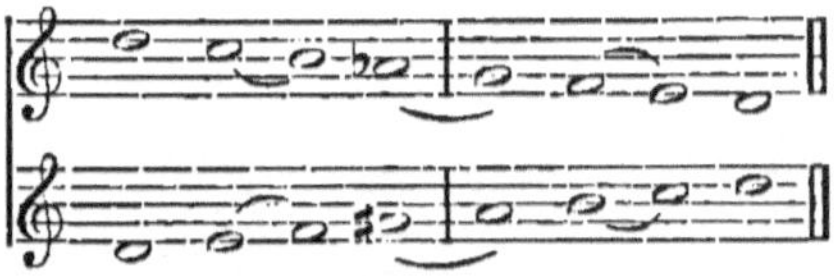

(15) Scales Nos. 115 and 87.

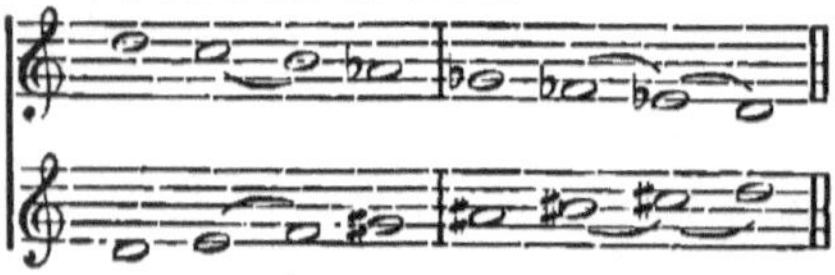

(16) Scales Nos. 116 and 86.

(17) Scales Nos. 118 and 90.

115. Nos. 117 and 88 by concurrence form a Double Counterpoint in the *Ninth;* and
116. The remaining Nos., 98 and 109, produce a Double Counterpoint in the *Thirteenth*, thus:—

EXAMPLE XLIV.
Scales Nos. 117 and 88.

EXAMPLE XLV.
Scales Nos. 98 and 109.

THE CHROMATIC GENUS.

117. One chromatic tetrachord now alone remains to complete the direct Oriental system of tonality. It is that of the diminished fourth form, a form of which we were furnished with two instances by the diatonic genus. Our readers will have observed, that of the twelve differing tetrachords six have been minor (and consonant), furnished equally, three and three, by each genus; and six have been major or diminished (and dissonant), furnished in the proportion of one and two in the diatonic to two and one in the chromatic genus. That final one, first developed in a transposed form in the second class of diatonic scales in Examples III. and V., here follows:—

EXAMPLE XLVI.

118. This final chromatic tetrachord, blended with the eleven tetrachords already treated of, brings up the present total of Chromatic scales to onehundred and eight, and the total in both orders to onehundred and fortyfour. The two scales (Nos. 125 and 136) of the second diatonic class in Example XXV., which were omitted because of the chromatic diminished tetrachord c d e f, are included in the following example of twentythree new octave scales.

EXAMPLE XLVII.

* This doublesharp is thus printed to economise space: it applies to both A and C.

* This doublesharp applies to both A and C. † This doubleflat applies to both E and G.

THE CHROMATIC GENUS. 49

119. Of these twentythree scales we are obliged to except five as unworkable, in each of which two cases of the diminished fourth concur. This brings up the number of exceptions to eighteen, which exceptions reduce the working scales to onehundred and twentysix. The five present excepted scales are Nos. 126, 127, 137, 138, and 144. No. 144 is alone capable of the Double Counterpoint inversion in the *Octave*, thus :—

EXAMPLE XLVIII.

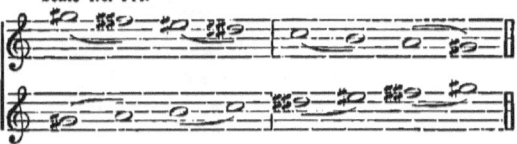

120. The above is the twelfth instance of pure Double Counterpoint in the *Octave*. The eighteen scales which follow, bring up the instances of the illegitimate Double Counterpoint in the same interval to fiftythree.

EXAMPLE XLIX.

* This doubleflat applies to both E and G.

H

(3) Scales Nos. 124 and 133.

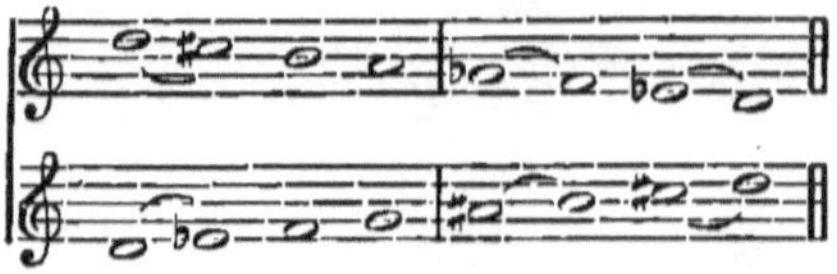

(4) Scales Nos. 126 and 138.

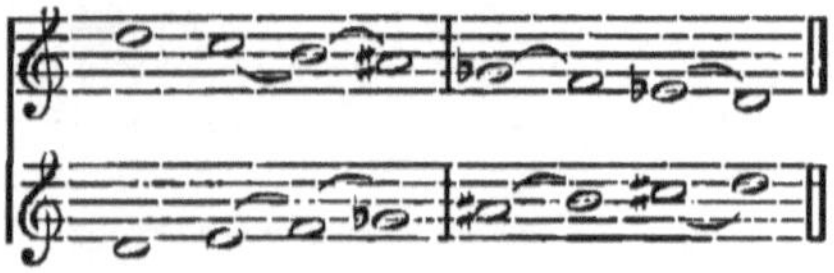

(5) Scales Nos. 128 and 139.

(6) Scales Nos. 130 and 140.

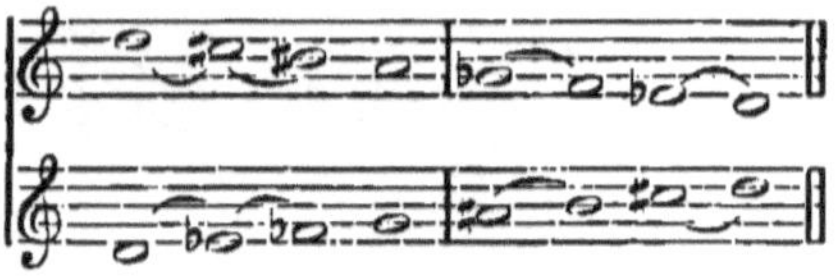

(7) Scales Nos. 131 and 143.

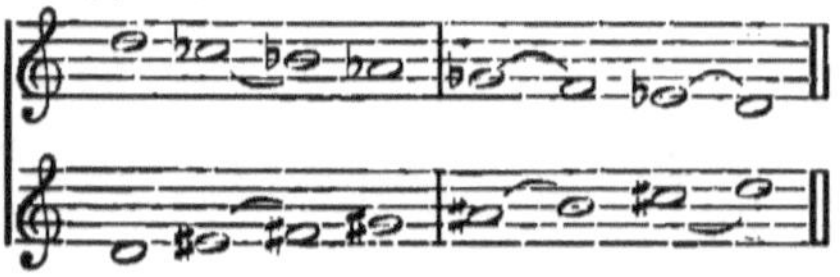

(8) Scales Nos. 132 and 142.

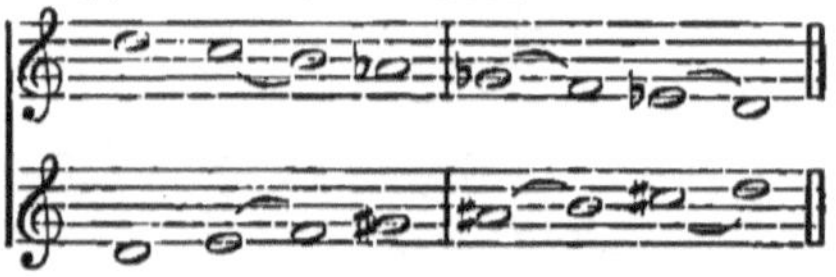

(9) Scales Nos. 137 and 127.

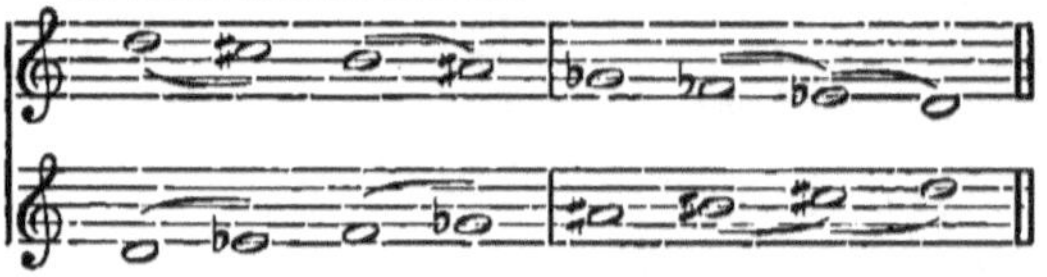

121. The instances of Double Counterpoint respectively in the

Ninth	have	been	five,
Tenth	"	"	two,
Eleventh	"	"	two.
Thirteenth	"	"	two.

122. Double Counterpoint in the *Twelfth* has as yet found no place: but in the present group of scales we at last come upon two instances thereof, the product of the junction of scales Nos. 125 and 129 with Nos. 136 and 141, which follow:—

EXAMPLE L.

(1) Scales Nos. 125 and 136.

(2) Scales Nos. 129 and 141.

THE CHROMATIC GENUS. 51

123. It is impossible to remark upon the multitudinous ramifications and involutions of which this array of scales is capable. To attempt the task within the moderate limits of a readable treatise would be foolishness itself; and could the attempt be successful, it might probably be deemed an invasion of the sanctuary of genius. But if we cannot show all that may be done, we will, in doing our little, point out what, from the foregoing, may be wisely eliminated, and also indicate the sources from whence compensation may be looked for.

124. And first, we will call attention to the fact that the onehundred and eight chromatic scales of Examples XXXVI., XLI., and XLVII., consist of two distinct orders (1) *pure*, in which both tetrachords are chromatic, and (2) *mixed*, in which one tetrachord is chromatic, the other diatonic.

125. So that in the foregoing lists, from Example III. onwards, we have thirtysix diatonic scales formed of tetrachords 1 to 6, of which scales five are unworkable,—Nos. 16, 25, 30, 35, and 36; thirtysix chromatic scales formed of tetrachords 7 to 12, of which scales also five are unworkable,—Nos. 100, 110, 120, 121, and 144; and seventytwo mixed diatonic and chromatic scales formed of tetrachords 1 to 6 interblended with tetrachords 7 to 12, of which scales eight are unworkable,—Nos. 85, 94, 104, 114, 126, 127, 137, and 138.

126. The eighteen unworkable scales contain, it will be remembered, one of the two impossible intervals: either (1) the diminished second, the two notes of which overlap each other instead of exhibiting a space or interval, as b-natural : c-flat in No. 16; or (2) the doubly-augmented second, which exceeds the interval of a major third, as g-natural : a-doublesharp in No. 25.

127. The three remaining seconds—minor, major, and augmented—are each workable, and form the material from which the two tetrachords in each of the onehundred and twentysix working scales are constructed. But though each of these onehundred and twentysix scales consist of workable intervals only, certain of their number are less desirable than the others, for the reason given in the three following paragraphs:—

128. In the formation of the twelve tetrachords which furnished us with the previous onehundred and fortyfour scales, it will be noticed that the three diminished fourth tetrachords of Examples XXVII. and XLVI. contain each two minor seconds and one major second; the three diatonic minor fourth tetrachords of Example II. contain each one minor second and two major seconds; the three chromatic minor fourth tetrachords of Example XXXV. contain each two minor seconds and one augmented second; the diatonic major fourth tetrachord of Example IV. contains three major seconds; and the two chromatic major fourth tetrachords of Example XL. contain each one minor second, one major second, and one augmented second.

129. The diatonic scales Nos. 1 to 15, 20, 24, 29, and 34; the semi-chromatic scales Nos. 23 and 26, with their augmented second tetrachordal junction; the chromatic scales Nos. 49, 88, 98, 109, 117, 129, 131, 141, and 143; the mixed diatonic and chromatic scales Nos. 37 to 40, 43 to 46, 53, 57, 67, 76, 82 to 84, 91, 95, 103, 106, 111 to 113, 122, 135, and the two which are virtually diatonic scales, Nos. 125 and 136, fiftysix in all, develop in their *internal incidence* none other than the twelve fundamental tetrachords which form the two halves of each scale.

130. But the remaining seventy working scales do not offer the same clear record when analysed. They afford us incidental instances of four additional chromatic major fourth tetrachords ($=4$); of one doubly-diminished fourth tetrachord ($4 + 1 = 5$); of six augmented fourth tetrachords ($5 + 6 = 11$); and of three doubly-augmented fourth tetrachords ($11 + 3 = 14$); making, with the previous twelve fundamental tetrachords, a total of twentysix existing tetrachords.

131. The four additional instances of the chromatic major fourth tetrachords are as workable and nearly as desirable as the two instances in Example XL., but being incidental only have no specific place, of right, in the chromatic scale, as have their fundamental brethren. Their inferiority to the two fundamental instances in Example XL. is due to the fact that the chromatic augmented second in each is either preceded or followed by a major second, thus involving, in three consecutive notes, the abnormal augmented third: while in the pure chromatic scale, with its semitonal neighbours on both sides, the augmented second involves, in three consecutive notes, the major third only. These new tetrachords, with the others which follow, constitute what may be styled a compound genus. We formulate each, for convenience, upon the natural major fourth interval (f-natural : b-natural), as follows:—

H 2

EXAMPLE LI.

132. Of these additional chromatic major fourth tetrachords, the first two are developed in four classes by scales Nos. 22, 66, and 75; 17, 105, and 116; 102, 132, and 134; 61, 69, and 81. The student is invited to prove this for himself by analysing each of those scales in manner following:—

EXAMPLE LII.

133. In the following list of fiftytwo scales of the compound genus, which covers the ground of the first two additional chromatic major fourth tetrachords, sixteen scales occur which are related to the twelve quoted in the previous paragraph, and three others (Nos. 152, 176, and 190), which will be referred to shortly. These nineteen scales we give in their order in the same manner as the onehundred and fortyfour based on the twelve fundamental tetrachords: but the remainder we indicate by letterpress only, making use of

Italic capitals	as A	to express	doublesharps,
Italic lower case letters	„ a	„	sharps,
Roman lower case letters	„ a	„	naturals,
Roman small capitals .	„ A	„	flats,
Roman large capitals .	„ A	„	doubleflats.

* In performance, attention must be paid to the signatural sharps and flats, which differ much from those in ordinary use.

THE CHROMATIC GENUS.

EXAMPLE LIII.

(148) Tet. 13 and 4. Two major fourths: unworkable.
(149) Tet. 13 and 5. E F G a | b c D E.
(150) Tet. 13 and 6. D E F g | a b c D.

(153) Tet. 13 and 9. D E F g | A b c D.
(154) Tet. 13 and 10. Two major fourths: unworkable.
(155) Tet. 13 and 11.   ,,   ,,   ,,
(156) Tet. 13 and 12. A B C d | e f g A.

(158) Tet. 2 and 13. d e f g | A B c d.
(159) Tet. 3 and 13. g a b c | D E F g.
(160) Tet. 4 and 13. Two major fourths: unworkable.

(162) Tet. 6 and 13. a b c D | E F G a.
(163) Tet. 7 and 13. g A b c | D E F g.

(165) Tet. 9 and 13. c d e f | G A B c.
(166) Tet. 10 and 13. Two major fourths: unworkable.
(167) Tet. 11 and 13.   ,,   ,,   ,,

(169) Tet. 13 and 13. Two major fourths: unworkable.
(170) Tet. 14 and 1. a b C d | e f g a.
(171) Tet. 14 and 2. g a b c | d e f g.

THE CHROMATIC GENUS.

134. The second two of the four additional chromatic major fourth tetrachords in Example LI. are developed, also in four classes, by scales Nos. 27, 50, and 58; 33, 86, and 96; 92, 123, and 142; 62, 64, and 70. We analyse one scale in each class, as before.

EXAMPLE LIV.

135. In the following list of sixty scales of the compound genus, which covers the ground of the second two of the four additional chromatic major fourth tetrachords, sixteen scales occur which are related to the twelve quoted in the previous paragraph, and three others (Nos. 205, 217, and 249), which will be referred to directly. These nineteen scales we give in their order, and the remainder we indicate by letterpress only, as in Example LIII.

EXAMPLE LV.

THE CHROMATIC GENUS.

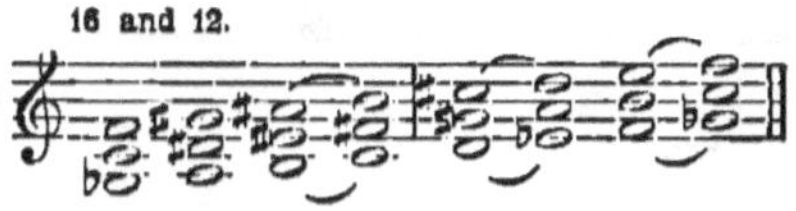

(237) **16 and 12.**

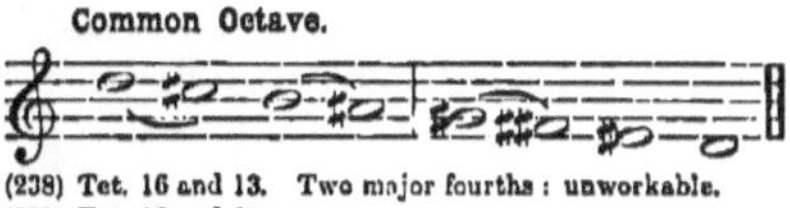

(238) Tet. 16 and 13. Two major fourths: unworkable.
(239) Tet. 16 and 14.   ,,   ,,   ,,
(240) Tet. 16 and 15.   ,,   ,,   ,,

(241) **1 and 16.**

(242) **2 and 16.**

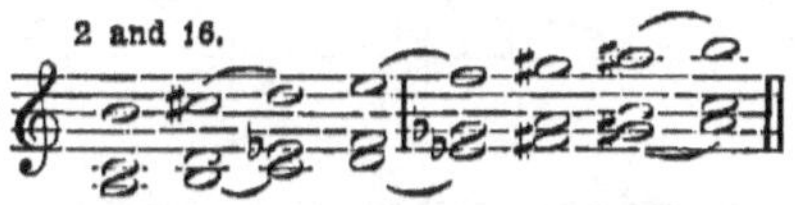

(243) **3 and 16.**

(244) Tet. 4 and 16. Two major fourths: unworkable.
(245) Tet. 5 and 16.   d e f g | a b C d.
(246) Tet. 6 and 16.   c d e f | g a b c.

(247) **7 and 16.**

(248) Tet. 8 and 16.   d e f g | a b C d.

(249) **9 and 16.**

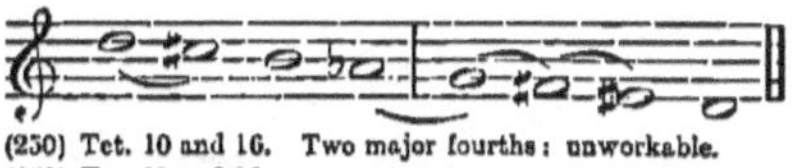

(250) Tet. 10 and 16. Two major fourths: unworkable.
(251) Tet. 11 and 16.   ,,   ,,   ,,
(252) Tet. 12 and 16. g a b c | d e F g.
(253) Tet. 13 and 16. Two major fourths: unworkable.
(254) Tet. 14 and 16.   ,,   ,,   ,,
(255) Tet. 15 and 16.   ,,   ,,   ,,
(256) Tet. 16 and 16.   ,,   ,,   ,,

Common Octave.

136. The one instance of the doubly-diminished fourth tetrachord, containing three minor seconds, which by its semitonal motion commends itself to Western ears as the ideal chromatic tetrachord, is developed in two classes by scales Nos. 79 and 119; 56 and 89, in the fundamental series, and by Nos. 152, 176, and 190; 205, 217, and 249, in the non-fundamental series at Examples LIII. and LV. Though in comparatively unfrequent use, and limited to one form, this doubly-diminished fourth tetrachord demands a place at our hands as both practicable and desirable. Its simplest and most normal definition is as follows, although it does not possess, of right, any specific place in the octave.

EXAMPLE LVI.

Tetrachord 17.

or

I

137. The analysis of one scale in each class, as in manner previous, shows the incidental development of the doubly-diminished fourth tetrachord, thus:—

138. In the following list of thirtythree scales of the compound genus, which covers the ground of the doubly-diminished fourth tetrachord, four scales only of that grade occur. These added to the six scales in Examples LIII. and LV., and to the four fundamental scales Nos. 56, 79, 89, and 119, make fourteen scales, or sufficient to complete the two classes or families of scales bearing this particular tetrachord. We confine ourselves, as before, to letterpress indication of the unquoted scales.

THE CHROMATIC GENUS.

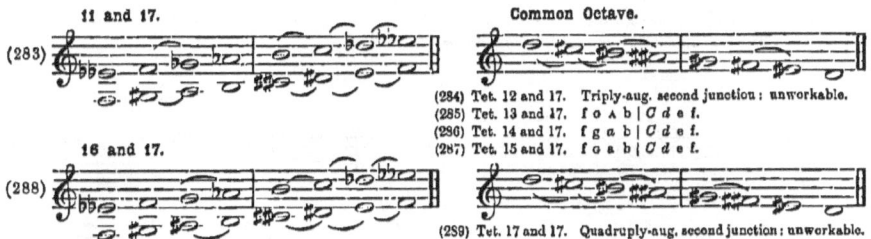

(284) Tet. 12 and 17. Triply-aug. second junction: unworkable.
(285) Tet. 13 and 17.   f o A b | C d e f.
(286) Tet. 14 and 17.   f g a b | C d e f.
(287) Tet. 15 and 17.   f o a b | C d e f.
(289) Tet. 17 and 17. Quadruply-aug. second junction: unworkable.

139. The five non-fundamental tetrachords (Nos. 13 to 17) developed thus far by the original series of onehundred and twentysix working scales, and the fortytwo new scales (19+19+4) of the compound genus based upon those tetrachords, have, it will be seen, proved themselves worthy of adoption, being both practicable and desirable, and are consequently adopted.

140. We will now, in the second place, glance at the remaining nine non-fundamental and less desirable tetrachords of the compound genus developed by the original series of scales, taking the six augmented fourth tetrachords and the three doubly-augmented fourth tetrachords in the order of their production, thus:—

EXAMPLE LIX.
AUGMENTED FOURTH TETRACHORDS.

141. No words are needed in proof of the assertion, that these nine tetrachords, though possible, are most difficult of performance. Still, as they find place in the original series of onehundred and twentysix working scales, it is not proper to ignore their existence. We will give an analysis, after the former manner, of one scale of the different classes in which each tetrachord is developed.

142. Tetrachord 18, the first of the augmented fourths, is developed by the two scales Nos. 18 and 32, representing each a class or family of scales.

EXAMPLE LX.

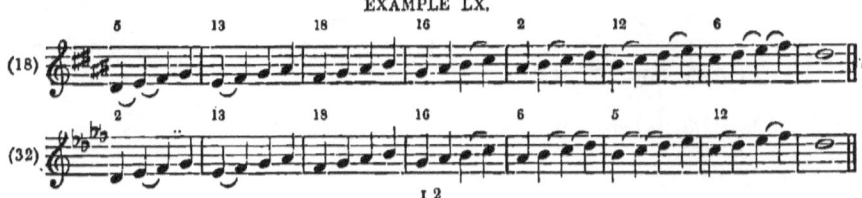

143. Tetrachord 19, the second of the augmented fourths, is developed by the nine scales Nos. 19; 28, 51, and 59; 52 and 60; 87, 93, and 124, in four classes, thus:—

EXAMPLE LXI.

144. Tetrachord 20, the third of the augmented fourths, is developed by the nine scales Nos. 21, 65, and 74; 31; 68 and 73; 101, 115, and 133, also in four classes, thus:—

EXAMPLE LXII.

145. Tetrachord 21, the fourth of the augmented fourths, is developed by the twelve scales Nos. 41, 71, 90, 97, 42; 47; 48, 63, 107, 118, and 139, in four classes, thus:—

EXAMPLE LXIII.

146. Tetrachords 22 and 23, the fifth and sixth of the augmented fourths, are developed by the seven scales Nos. 54, 72, and 78; 99 and 130; 108 and 140, in three classes, thus:—

EXAMPLE LXIV.

147. Tetrachord 24, the first of the doubly-augmented fourths, is developed by scale No. 55 only, thus:—

EXAMPLE LXV.

148. Tetrachord 25, the second of the doubly-augmented fourths, is developed by scale No. 77 only, thus:—

EXAMPLE LXVI.

149. Tetrachord 26, the third of the doubly-augmented fourths, is developed by scale No. 80 only, thus:—

EXAMPLE LXVII.

150. It will be seen that the number of undesirable scales $(2 + 9 + 9 + 12 + 7 + 1 + 1 + 1 = 42)$ of the original series, governed by the tetrachords 18 to 26, at Examples LX. to LXVII., exactly balances the fortytwo new scales brought in by the new series at Examples LIII., LV., and LVIII. So that if we exclude the former altogether, and take in their place the fortytwo new scales, we still have onehundred and twentysix working scales as in the original series, but with the additional satisfaction that all are alike practicable and desirable.

151. As the onehundred and twentysix working scales stood originally, they represented thirtyeight classes or families of scales with varying numbers of instances in the classes. Thus there were:—

	8 classes with	7 instances each	=	56 scales.
	2 „	5 „	„ =	10 „
	13 „	3 „	„ =	39 „
	6 „	2 „	„ =	12 „
	9 „	1 instance	„ =	9 „
Total = 38	„	. . .	.	126 „

152. But by purging the series of—

	2 . .	classes with 5 instances each	= 10 scales.
	5 of the 13	„ 3 „	„ = 15 „
	4 „ 6	„ 2 „	„ = 8 „
	9 . .	„ 1 instance	„ = 9 „
In all, 20		„ . .	. 42 „

which contain the undesirable augmented and doubly-augmented fourth tetrachords of Examples LX. to LXVII., and by adding in their stead the fortytwo new scales of Examples LIII., LV., and LVIII., we have eighteen full classes or families of scales with seven instances each, which are equal to the original total of onehundred and twentysix working scales, thus:—$18 \times 7 = 126$.

153. These fortytwo new scales of the compound genus, though unresolvable any two of them into a common sequence of reversible intervals, are yet susceptible of the illegitimate kind of Double Counterpoint in the *Octave* of Example XXX., and raise the number of instances of that kind, which in Example XLIX. stood at fiftythree, to seventyfour.

EXAMPLE LXVIII.

(1) Scales Nos. 145 and 243.   (2) Scales Nos. 146 and 242.

PART IV.—CLASSIFICATION OF SCALES.

THE point has now been reached when we can classify aright the onehundred and twentysix working scales, having (1) pruned off sundry of the more undesirable members, and (2) filled up the gaps which existed in ten of the original classes or families of scales.

155. Taken seriatim, the onehundred and twentysix working scales, after this necessary pruning and filling up, stand as follows:—

Nos. 1, 2, 3, 4, 5, 6, 7, 8, 9, 10, 11, 12, 13, 14,
„ 15, 17, 20, 22, 23, 24, 26, 27, 29, 33, 34, 37, 38, 39,
„ 40, 43, 44, 45, 46, 49, 50, 53, 56, 57, 58, 61, 62, 64,
„ 66, 67, 69, 70, 75, 76, 79, 81, 82, 83, 84, 86, 88, 89,
„ 91, 92, 95, 96, 98, 102, 103, 105, 106, 109, 111, 112, 113, 116,
„ 117, 119, 122, 123, 125, 129, 131, 132, 134, 135, 136, 141, 142, 143,
„ 145, 146, 147, 151, 152, 157, 161, 164, 168, 172, 175, 176, 178, 181,
„ 183, 184, 185, 189, 190, 197, 198, 199, 203, 205, 211, 215, 217, 218,
„ 222, 228, 231, 234, 237, 241, 242, 243, 247, 249, 266, 269, 283, 288.

They form, as before observed, eighteen classes or families with seven instances each.

156. To enable our readers to test more readily the representative scales of the eighteen classes or families, analysed in alternate Examples LXX. to CIV., we bring together in one view the various tetrachords of which they are composed, from Examples II., IV., XXVII., XXXV., XL., XLVI., LI., and LVI., thus:—

EXAMPLE LXIX.
DIATONIC TETRACHORDS.

CHROMATIC TETRACHORDS.

COMPOUND TETRACHORDS.

157. CLASS 1, with which we have already made acquaintance in Example XXIV., contains, as will be seen in the following analysis of a representative scale of the class, two instances of each of the three diatonic minor fourth tetrachords of Example II., and one instance of the diatonic major fourth tetrachord of Example IV., as follows :—

EXAMPLE LXX.

158. Everything in this Example is perfectly natural, and the family of seven scales governed thereby, is, as previously explained, the foundation of the Western Gregorian system, as well as that of the Oriental diatonic genus.

EXAMPLE LXXI.
CLASS 1.

159. CLASS 2, in great part displayed at Example XXV., which requires for its normal definition one sharp (c) or one flat (E), contains four diatonic minor fourth tetrachords, No. 2 being doubled; two diatonic major fourth tetrachords; and one transposed chromatic diminished fourth tetrachord of Example XLVI., as follows :—

EXAMPLE LXXII.

160. While in Class 1 the dissonant tritonal major fourth tetrachord was entirely subordinated by the presence of the six consonant minor fourth tetrachords, in this second class it asserts itself more strongly, being doubled; and the diminished fourth tetrachord still further separates the present class from the absolute purity of Class 1. As before observed, the above representative scale, No. 8, was formerly the ascending form of the Minor mode.

EXAMPLE LXXIII.
CLASS 2.

161. CLASS 3, displayed in part only at Example XXVI., which requires for its normal definition two sharps (c and d) or two flats (E and D), contains two diatonic minor fourth tetrachords only, No. 2 being omitted; three diatonic major fourth tetrachords; and the two diatonic diminished fourth tetrachords of Example XXVII., as follows:—

EXAMPLE LXXIV.

162. The dissonant tritonal major fourth tetrachord here occupies the leading place, three instances occurring to two of the consonant minor fourth tetrachord. The two diminished fourth tetrachords also help to overshadow the consonant tetrachords. This is as far as a family of diatonic scales can be expected to wander from purity.

EXAMPLE LXXV.
CLASS 3.

163. CLASS 4, the Oriental chromatic scale in its fundamental form, requires for its normal definition two sharps (g and d) or two flats (A and D). It has no internal incidence of the diatonic tetrachords of the three previous families of scales, but introduces us instead to an entirely new series; giving us four chromatic minor fourth tetrachords of Example XXXV., No. 7 being doubled; the two chromatic major fourth tetrachords of Example XL.; and the one chromatic diminished fourth tetrachord of Example XLVI., as follows:—

EXAMPLE LXXVI.

164. Notwithstanding that we are landed on quite a new musical territory, dispensing altogether with the tetrachords of the primitive diatonic scales, there are few who will not admit, after a short experience, that the family of scales now about to follow not only possesses a character intrinsically its own, but also carries with it a promise of possibilities as yet unattained, or even unimagined.

EXAMPLE LXXVII.
CLASS 4.

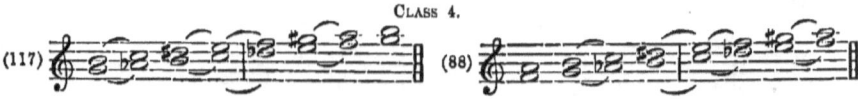

CLASSIFICATION OF SCALES. 69

165. The four classes next in order, Nos. 5 to 8, are formed of a mixture of the diatonic and chromatic genuses, and include under their standard or gauge the great bulk of Oriental music.

166. CLASS 5, which requires for its normal definition one sharp (g) or two flats (E and A), contains one each of the three diatonic minor fourth tetrachords; one chromatic minor fourth tetrachord, No. 7, the norm; the two chromatic major fourth tetrachords; and the one chromatic diminished fourth tetrachord, as follows in what has been previously alluded to as the most modern fashion of the Minor mode:—

EXAMPLE LXXVIII.

167. This small modicum of the Oriental chromatic genus, having been already accepted by the Western musical world, needs no eulogy in this place. We only hope that other portions, equally worthy and equally pleasing, will also soon obtain acceptance.

EXAMPLE LXXIX.
CLASS 5.

168. CLASS 6, which requires for its normal definition two sharps (c and g) or one flat (A), consists of the same tetrachords as Class 5, disposed as follows:—

EXAMPLE LXXX.

169. Though the tetrachords are the same as those in Example LXXVII., their different order induces a great difference of character in the two families of scales.

EXAMPLE LXXXI.
CLASS 6.

170. CLASS 7, which requires for its normal definition one sharp (d) or three flats (E, A, and D), contains, of the diatonic genus, two minor fourth tetrachords (No. 2 being omitted), the one major fourth tetrachord, and one diminished fourth tetrachord; and of the chromatic genus, two minor fourth tetrachords, and one major fourth tetrachord, as follows:—

EXAMPLE LXXXII.

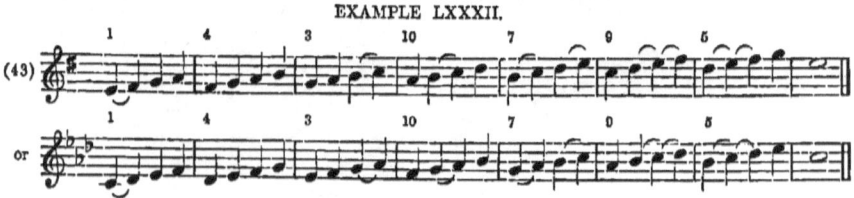

CLASSIFICATION OF SCALES.   71

171. Although the diatonic genus has prevailed over the chromatic to the extent of four to three, yet the loss of one diatonic minor fourth tetrachord contained in Examples LXXVIII. and LXXX. makes it that as compared with their two families at Examples LXXIX. and LXXXI., the family following is slightly less pure than they.

EXAMPLE LXXXIII.
Class 7

172. Class 8, which requires for its normal definition three sharps (c, g, and d) or one flat (D), consists of the same generic order of tetrachords as Class 7, though not of the same individual instances: Nos. 6; 8, and 11 taking the places of Nos. 5; 9, and 10; while Nos. 1, 3, 4; and 7 remain unaltered, as follows:—

EXAMPLE LXXXIV.

173. The same remark which applied to the previous family at paragraph 171 applies also to the following, which exhausts the list of fiftysix scales enumerated at paragraph 129.

EXAMPLE LXXXV.
Class 8.

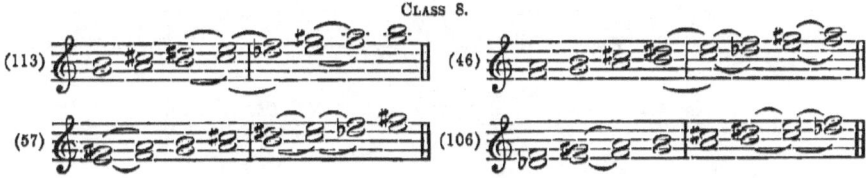

174. We have now exhausted the scales based upon the diatonic tetrachords Nos. 1 to 6, and the chromatic tetrachords Nos. 7 to 12. The ten remaining families of scales admit of yet a third series of tetrachords, Nos. 13 to 17, neither diatonic nor chromatic, but a compound of both genuses.

175. CLASS 9, which requires for its normal definition one sharp (a) or four flats (E, A, D, and G), contains, of the diatonic genus, the three minor fourth tetrachords, and one diminished fourth tetrachord; of the chromatic genus, one minor fourth tetrachord; and of the compound genus, the first two major fourth tetrachords of Example LI., as follows :—

EXAMPLE LXXXVI.

176. Only for the presence of the two compound tetrachords Nos. 13 and 14, the following family would claim, from the fact of possessing the three consonant diatonic minor fourth tetrachords, a higher degree of purity than the two families immediately preceding.

EXAMPLE LXXXVII.

CLASS 9.

177. CLASS 10, which requires for its normal definition four sharps (c, g, d, and a) or one flat (G), consists of the same generic order of tetrachords as Class 9, though not of the same individual instances: Nos. 6; 8; and the third and fourth tetrachords of the compound genus at Example LI, Nos. 15 and 16, taking the places of Nos. 5; 9; 13, and 14: while Nos. 1, 2, and 3 remain unaltered, as follows:—

EXAMPLE LXXXVIII.

178. This family, being its true correlative, has the same claim to superiority as Class 9 over its two immediate predecessors at Examples LXXXIII. and LXXXV.

EXAMPLE LXXXIX.
CLASS 10.

179. CLASS 11, which requires for its normal definition three sharps (c, d, and a) or two flats (A and G), contains, of the diatonic genus, two minor fourth tetrachords (No. 2 being omitted), and the two diminished fourth tetrachords; of the chromatic genus, one major fourth tetrachord; and of the compound genus, the first two major tetrachords of Example LI., as follows:—

EXAMPLE XC.

L

180. We are here less influenced than in Classes 9 and 10 by the consonant diatonic minor fourth tetrachords, and consequently have lost somewhat more in purity.

EXAMPLE XCI.
CLASS 11.

181. CLASS 12, which requires for its normal definition two sharps (g and a) or three flats (E, D, and G), consists of the same generic order of tetrachords as Class 11, though not of the same individual instances: Nos. 10; 15, and 16 taking the places of Nos. 11; 13, and 14: while Nos. 1, 3, 5, and 6 remain unaltered, as follows:—

EXAMPLE XCII.

182. This, being the true correlative of Class 11, appropriates to itself the remark at paragraph 180.

EXAMPLE XCIII.
CLASS 12.

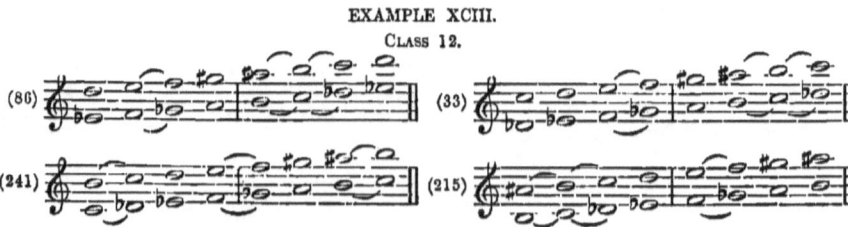

183. CLASS 13, which requires for its normal definition two sharps (*c* and *a*) or three flats (E, A, and G), contains, of the diatonic genus, two minor fourth tetrachords, No. 2 being doubled; of the chromatic genus, one major fourth tetrachord, and the diminished fourth tetrachord doubled; and of the compound genus, the first two major fourth tetrachords of Example LI., as follows:—

EXAMPLE XCIV.

184. The doubling of tetrachords 2 and 12 gives to this family a piquant air less observable in sundry others of greater accredited purity.

EXAMPLE XCV.
CLASS 13.

185. CLASS 14, which requires for its normal definition three sharps (*c*, *g*, and *a*) or two flats (E and G), consists of the same generic order of tetrachords as Class 13, though not of the same individual instances: Nos. 10; 15, and 16 taking the places of Nos. 11; 13, and 14: while Nos. 2; and 12 remain unaltered, as follows:—

EXAMPLE XCVI.

186. The remark at paragraph 184 applies to the following also, as its true correlative.

EXAMPLE XCVII.
Class 14.

187. Class 15, which requires for its normal definition two sharps (d and a) or three flats (A, D, and G), contains, of the diatonic genus, one diminished fourth tetrachord; of the chromatic genus, four minor fourth tetrachords, No. 9 being doubled; and of the compound genus, the first two major fourth tetrachords of Example LI., as follows:—

EXAMPLE XCVIII.

188. We have here the greatest departure from purity we have yet experienced. The all-but absence of the diatonic genus, and the subordinate position of the principal chromatic minor fourth tetrachord No. 7, remove it farther than any previous family from accepted Western ideals.

CLASSIFICATION OF SCALES.

EXAMPLE XCIX.
Class 15.

[musical examples labelled (61), (81), (189), (164), (69), (178), (151)]

189. CLASS 16, which requires for its normal definition three sharps (*g*, *d*, and *a*) or two flats (D and G), consists of the same generic order of tetrachords as Class 15, though not of the same individual instances: Nos. 6; 8-8, 9; 15, and 16 taking the places of Nos. 5; 8, 9-9; 13, and 14: while No. 7 alone remains unaltered, as follows:—

EXAMPLE C.

190. This class, as its true correlative, shares with Class 15 in the remark at paragraph 188 respecting the increased departure from purity. But, it must not be forgotten, that the greater or less departure from normal purity, on which we remarked when treating earlier on the diatonic genus, has as little practical effect here as there.

EXAMPLE CI.
Class 16.

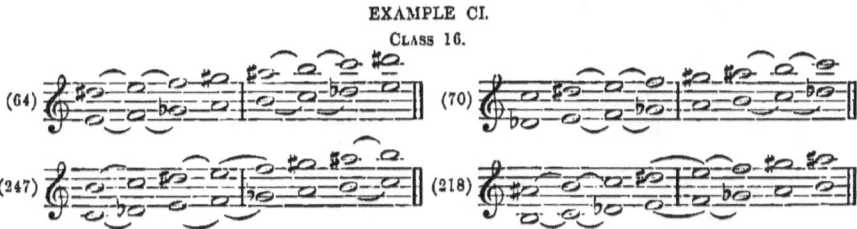

191. A tetrachord of quite a different form from any yet tabulated now makes its appearance in the non-fundamental series of the compound genus. It is formed of the doubly-diminished fourth, an interval not to be confounded with the true sesquitone, the minor third, seeing that, though it consists of three semitones only, those three semitones are each of them major. Yet the anomaly of our preliminary pages here also asserts itself, and this nominal fourth, formed of three major semitones, is of smaller extent than the sesquitone, whose three semitones are two of them major and one minor. Thus, while the latter, as before mentioned at paragraph 13, is represented by the proportion 27 : 32, which multiplied by 531441 (to assimilate the forms of reckoning) is equal to

$$14348907 : 17006112,$$

the former or diminished fourth is represented by

$$14348907 : 16777216,$$

a deficiency of nearly one and a half per cent.

192. CLASS 17, which requires for its normal definition two sharps and one doublesharp (g, d, and C) or three flats and one doubleflat (A, D, G, and E), contains, of the chromatic genus, the three minor fourth tetrachords, and one major fourth tetrachord; and of the compound genus, the first two major fourth tetrachords of Example LI., and the doubly-diminished fourth tetrachord of Example LVI., as follows:—

EXAMPLE CII.

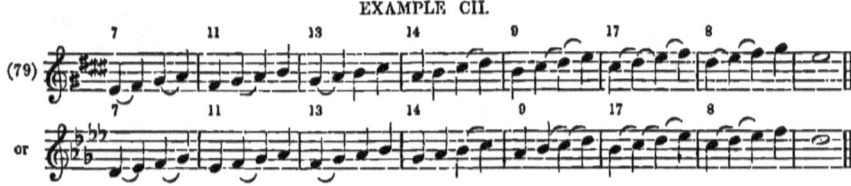

193. We have before observed that this doubly-diminished fourth tetrachord is the most like, in consequence of its semitonal construction, to the Western ideal of chromaticism. The entire absence of the diatonic genus from the internal incidence of the two families of scales governed by it, will also help the impression that their octave scales are, or deserve to be, in the same category.

EXAMPLE CIII.
CLASS 17.

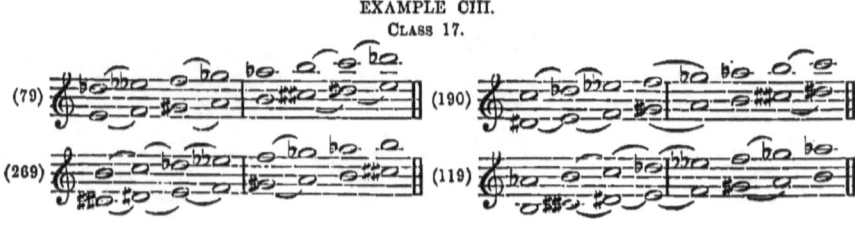

194. CLASS 18, which requires for its normal definition three sharps and one double-sharp (*g, d, a,* and *C*) or two flats and one double-flat (A, D, and E), consists of the same generic order of tetrachords as Class 17, though not of the same individual instances: Nos. 10; 15, and 16 taking the places of Nos. 11; 13, and 14; while Nos. 7, 8, 9; and 17 remain unaltered, as follows:—

EXAMPLE CIV.

195. The family now to follow brings us to the limit of the onehundred and twentysix selected scales which constitute the better workable portion of the tonal wealth of the Oriental musician.

EXAMPLE CV.
CLASS 18.

80　　　　　　　　　　BYZANTINE MUSIC.

106. Before leaving the question of classification, we will designate by name certain portions of the four classes of the mixed diatonic and chromatic scales in Examples LXXIX, LXXXI, LXXXIII, and LXXXV, as we did the fifteen workable diatonic scales in Examples XXIV, XXV, and XXVI. It will be observed that the diatonic tetrachord giving name to each of the following scales is the left hand or fundamental tetrachord. When that tetrachord is omitted, and the chromatic tetrachord occupies its place, the omitted tetrachord is still considered, and the scale, by developing upwards, Gregorian fashion, is regarded as a *Hyper* of the omitted fundamental tetrachordal scale.

EXAMPLE CVI.
ORIENTAL MIXED DIATONIC AND CHROMATIC SCALES.

CLASSIFICATION OF SCALES. 81

Hyper Chromatic Mixolydian Mode.
Common Octave.

(84)

Hyper Chromatic Hypodorian Mode.

(37)

Hyper Chromatic Hypolydian Mode.

(39)

197. If the question be asked—Why, in a series of normal scales, is the chromatic tetrachord of Scale No. 112, *The Chromatic Phrygian Mode*, a transposed and not a normal one? the answer is: Scale No. 112 has for its limits two natural D's. The normal chromatic scale No. 49, though it contains d-flat and d-sharp respectively in its two forms, possesses no d-natural.* To obtain that note transposition is necessary. The transposition of the different chromatic tetrachords for the obtaining that note is as follows:—

EXAMPLE CVII.

198. A short glance at the foregoing series of transposed chromatic tetrachords will at once convince us of the unerring instinct which led the old musicians to select as the missing link in this case the major fourth tetrachord No. 11, of which an incidental proof will be given in paragraph 274, later on. Tetrachord No. 11 is the only one which, ending in d-natural, can be written with one accidental character. Five of the other tetrachords require each two such characters and one of them three. This tetrachord No. 11 has, moreover, the honour of forming the chromatic half of the *Hypo* of its Mode, an honour otherwise peculiar to No. 7, the normal tetrachord.

* It is curious that d-natural, the most fertile note of the diatonic genus, should be altogether excluded from the chromatic genus.

M

PART V.—APPLICATION AND SPECIMENS.

IN proceeding to the practical application of the foregoing, by exhibiting and analyzing a few Specimens of musical composition, ancient and modern, based upon the different Oriental diatonic and chromatic scales, it may be as well to forewarn the reader not to expect generally long and elaborate instances of melody and harmony. The eastern nations are essentially conservative, and cherish with great affection the inheritance of their forefathers. Those forefathers, it may be presumed, were even a shade more simple and natural than their present successors, and the old music handed down from them is, of necessity, also simple. A complete melody will often be found to consist of one phrase only, many times repeated, and traversing (as will also longer melodies of ancient type) a scale of most limited proportions, sometimes of two or three notes only. Scales of four and five notes give comparative freedom and variety. The following Russian choral-dance consists of merely three measures of two crotchet time, and has a scale limit of five notes, from d-natural to a-natural. It is played through, as it stands, twentyone times.

EXAMPLE CVIII.
CHOROVODNAHYAH, OR CHORAL-DANCE, OF SEMENOFF, NIZHEGOROD, SUNG IN UNISON.

200. The reader will observe the simplicity of the accompaniment, which consists of a pedal or drone capable of being sustained by the two lower strings of a violin, or by two horns, while a flute or clarionet gives every alternate strain in octave canon at half measure distance. This latter is a worthy conception of the Russian mind.

201. We will now offer a few Specimens in the different Oriental modes, commencing with THE NATURAL DIATONIC SERIES.

202. THE DORIAN MODE, OR TONE I.

This mode, identical with the Gregorian Phrygian mode, or Tone 3, has ever been a favourite in the Church, and we find consequently that the bulk of music in existence based thereon is ecclesiastical. Modern church-writers are

APPLICATION AND SPECIMENS. 83

also not insensible to its merits, though they have utilized it far less than might have been expected from its singularly felicitous effect. Mendelssohn, in the Duet, No. 3, of his Oratorio *Elijah*, gives an ancient melody, of the compass of three notes only, to the Choral refrain "LORD, bow Thine Ear to our prayer," in this mode; while Handel has written therein the fugal Chorus "Egypt was glad," in Part I. of his Oratorio *Israel in Egypt*. A few secular compositions are to be found, and we give one such, with four of the religious order. Each example is given in its normal untransposed form; and the secular songs and choruses are printed without preludes or interludes,* for saving of space. Those who desire the altitudinal effect intended by the respective editors quoted, will find indications given in foot-notes whereby the different examples can be re-transposed.

EXAMPLE CIX.

LESSER INTROIT, FROM SUNDAY LITURGY OF THE RUSSIAN CHURCH, FOR FOUR VOICES.
(*Complete in One Stanza.*)

* No loss is sustained by this omission, as preludes and interludes form no part of the songs and choruses proper. We shall see, later on, that sometimes they are written in a different mode from that of the song or chorus with which they are associated, in which cases they are worse than useless for our purpose of illustration, being deceptive. A good accompanist is quite competent to form his own preludes and interludes.

M 2

EXAMPLE CX.
ALLELUIA OF THE APOSTLE, FROM LITURGY OF THE RUSSIAN CHURCH, FOR FOUR VOICES.
(Complete in One Stanza.)

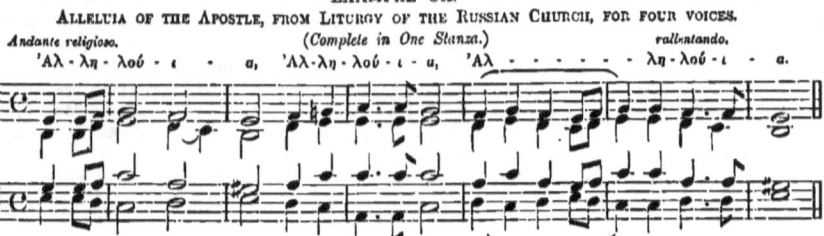

EXAMPLE CXI.
CHORUS FROM THE ORATORIETTE "BAPTISM," REDUCED FROM EIGHT TO FOUR VOICES.
(Complete in One Stanza.)

EXAMPLE CXII.
A LOVER'S SONG, OF SMYRNA.
(Complete in Two Stanzas.)

APPLICATION AND SPECIMENS. 85

EXAMPLE CXIII.
TRIUMPHAL HYMN, FROM COPTIC LITURGY OF ST. BASIL, FOR FOUR VOICES.
(Complete in One Stanza.)

BYZANTINE MUSIC.

203. The four notes of which Examples CIX. and CX. are formed constitute the fundamental tetrachord of this mode.

EXAMPLE CXIV.
No. 1.

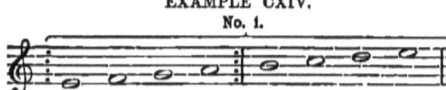

These examples are very fine specimens of the mode, and are a relic of the ecclesiastical music planted in Kieff by the Greek Christian missionaries on the conversion of Russia in the tenth century. The limited compass witnesses to their antiquity.

204. Example CXI. is taken from the present writer's Exercise or Thesis for the Oxford degree of Doctor of Music, entitled *Baptism: an Oratoriette* (London: R. Cocks & Co., 1860), in which it was preceded by two other numbers in the same mode.* It is here reduced to four parts for simplicity's sake, and for better comparison with other specimens, from the eight parts in which the Choral numbers of a Doctor's Exercise are always written. The example traverses the whole compass of the octave in this mode.

* Possessors of this volume will observe that the writer used in the Preface the current Western mode of reckoning when he says—"The musician versed in the ancient tonality will observe in Nos. 8, 9, and 10, specimens of the Phrygian mode; and in No. 13, a more largely developed instance of the massive Dorian mode." A better acquaintance with Oriental affairs, including Music, than was possible in 1860, obliges him now to invert the words *Phrygian* and *Dorian* in the above passage.

APPLICATION AND SPECIMENS. 87

EXAMPLE CXV.
No. 1.

205. Example CXII., *A Lover's Song*, taken from M. Bourgault-Ducoudray's *Trente Melodies Populaires de Grèce et d'Orient*,* No. 14,† is a good instance of secular use of this mode. It occupies the six lower notes of the authentic scale, and one note below its limit. This one note below the authentic limit makes it that the example occupies also the five upper notes of the plagal scale.

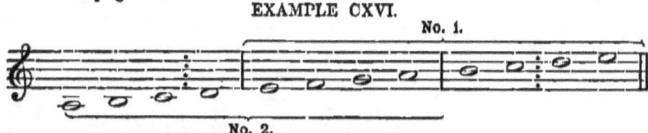

EXAMPLE CXVI.
No. 1.
No. 2.

But not only do the six authentic notes prevail in point of number over the five plagal ones to constitute an authentic melody, it is also always held that one extra note in either direction is not considered a disqualification of a melody from taking rank in the mode or scale furnishing the remainder of the notes. This rule we shall have further occasion to quote and act upon. The reader will find this simple melody grow upon acquaintance.

206. Example CXIII., from *The Scottish Review* of April, 1890, page 356, like Example CXII., trespasses one note below the limit of the authentic scale, which trespass gives, to this melody also, five plagal notes. But the melody ascends through seven notes of the diatonic scale, thus increasing its balance to seven against five.

EXAMPLE CXVII.
No. 1.
No. 2.

This example is of greater length and development than either of the preceding. In explanation of the fact of its commencement upon c-natural, the sixth of the scale, while it might be sufficient to say that c-natural is always held to be the dominant reciting note of the Gregorian 3rd tone, which agrees with our present mode, we beg to state that the example before us is a fragment only, and that the introductory part, consisting of nineteen unmistakably Dorian measures, is omitted. The words of *The Scottish Review* on this example may be here repeated:—"Different though it be to the received Greek and Latin forms of this hymn, there can be no question that the above is as beautiful as it is venerable. Few can enter into its spirit and not be moved thereby."

207. THE HYPODORIAN MODE, OR PLAGAL TONE I.

This mode agrees with the natural Minor mode, and, excepting that it originates in e-natural instead of d-natural, with the Hypodorian mode or Tone 2 of the Gregorian system. Like all plagal modes it may end either with its own final, or a fifth above, with the final of its parent authentic mode. This gives to the plagal modes an elasticity which the parent authentic modes, closing only with their own final, cannot possess. But this elasticity gives a vagueness which contrasts with the simplicity and directness of the authentic modes. We submit four widely differing specimens in support of this assertion, the three latter of which are taken from Mr. M. Balakiroff's *Sbornik Roosskikh Narodnikh Peysen* (St. Petersburg: A. Iohansen), Nos. 40, 4, and 5.

---

* It is proper to state that the specimens headed "of Smyrna" are given by M. Ducoudray on the authority of Madame Laffon.
† This song is transposed by M. Ducoudray a minor third higher.

EXAMPLE CXVIII.
Easter Hymn, from Service of the Greek Church, for four voices.
(Complete in One Stanza.)

EXAMPLE CXIX.
Boorlatskahyah, or Boatmen's Song, of Nizhni-Novgorod.*

(Complete in One Stanza.)

* Transposed a minor fifth higher.

APPLICATION AND SPECIMENS. 89

EXAMPLE CXX.
PROTIAZHNAUYAH, OR CONTINUOUS SONG, OF PRAMZEENAH, SIMBIRSK.*
(*Repeated in Eighteen Stanzas.*)

* Transposed a minor third lower.

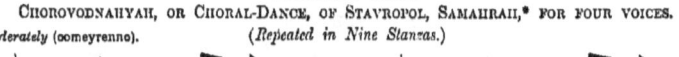

EXAMPLE CXXI.

Chorovodnahyah, or Choral-Dance, of Stavropol, Samahrah,* for four voices.

(Repeated in Nine Stanzas.)

* Transposed a minor second lower.

APPLICATION AND SPECIMENS. 91

208. Example CXVIII. is an ancient Greek ecclesiastical melody, taken from page 31 of the fourth or musical edition of Dr. Neale's *Hymns of the Eastern Church* * (London: J. T. Hayes, 1882), and is framed upon the lower trichord of each of the two Dorian tetrachords of scale No. 1, in inverse order, which form a series of six notes beautifully balanced in the Hypodorian scale, No. 2, thus:

EXAMPLE CXXII.

No. 2.

The harmony, it will be observed, is a little free, and does not confine itself strictly to the mode in the central six measures.

209. Example CXIX. covers the six upper notes of the plagal mode, and two notes above its limit. Conversely it may be said that it covers the six lower notes of the authentic mode, and two notes below *its* limit. This, for the moment, seems to make the claim of both modes equal.

EXAMPLE CXXIII.

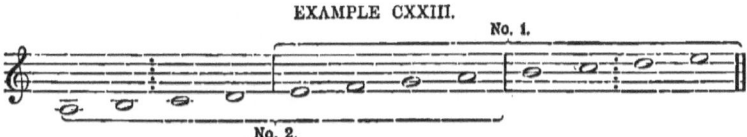

But a glance at the scale just given shows, that while the six authentic notes (being the two upper notes joined to the adjacent tetrachord) make a minor sixth only, the six plagal notes (being the two lower notes joined to the adjacent tetrachord) make a major sixth, thus giving by an extra semitone of dimension the preponderance to the plagal side. The prominent position held by a-natural throughout confirms the decision thus arrived at by calculation. The example is a capital specimen of the *Barcarole* class of song. It is slow and steady, like the Russian natural temperament, and is considerably less jerky than the ordinary six-quaver Italian form. The commencement on the plagal seventh, or third authentic, is not common; and the close takes the form of an imperfect cadence on the authentic final.

210. Example CXX. is a specimen of the Continuous-song so popular among the Russian peasantry, in which the various stanzas are joined by a small *codetta* at the close of the tune, which *codetta* is omitted at the last stanza when no longer needed. The present example is formed of the six lower notes of the plagal mode, and one note below its limit, or of the six upper notes of the authentic mode, and one note above *its* limit, thus:—

EXAMPLE CXXIV.

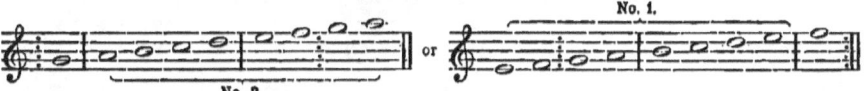

Treating it as we did the last example by adding the extra note of each mode to its adjacent tetrachord, we find that in the authentic mode we arrive at the interval of a minor fifth, while in the plagal mode we arrive at the interval of a major fifth, thus demonstrating the superior claim of the latter by the same semitonal gain as before. The prominent part again taken up by the a-natural, and still more its close on that note, determine the matter in favour of the plagal mode. The commencement on the plagal fourth, or seventh authentic, is very suggestive of old manner; and the close takes the well-known form of the plagal cadence on its final.

* Where it is transposed a major fifth higher.

211. Example CXXI. furnishes the greatest instance of vagueness we have yet experienced in these specimens. The melody occupies the complete course of the authentic mode, minus f-natural, yet its close is on the final of the plagal mode.

EXAMPLE CXXV.
No. 1.

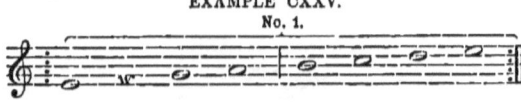

Whence arises this anomaly? The answer we will supply later on; and will now proceed to

212. THE PHRYGIAN MODE, OR TONE II.

This mode answers to the Gregorian Dorian mode, or Tone 1, and is the mode on which the first of the two Chants in Example XVI. is based. It is bold and striking in its effect, and was the first mode popularised in the West by harmonic treatment. Tallis and the first English Church composers exulted in this mode. Handel has written therein the *Alla Capella* fugal Chorus "And I will exalt Him," in Part II. of his Oratorio *Israel in Egypt*. Among the ancient Greeks this Phrygian mode was credited with "the power of inspiration," while to the first or Dorian mode was attributed "the qualities of repose and dignity," since "it was considered to be the only one calculated to inspire respect for the law, obedience, courage, self-esteem, and independence." * We furnish three examples.

EXAMPLE CXXVI.
A LOVER'S SONG, OF SMYRNA.†
(Repeated in Three Stanzas.)

---

* Aristotle and the Spartan Ephori, quoted in Naumann's *History of Music*, page 134.
† *Ducoudray*, No. 11. Transposed a minor third higher.   ‡ Any other name may be here inserted.

APPLICATION AND SPECIMENS. 93

EXAMPLE CXXVII.

Coryphæus.   A PYTHIAN ODE, BY PINDAR.* SOLO, AND CHORUS FOR FOUR VOICES.
Un poco mosso.   (*Complete in One Stanza.*)

Chorus of Citharodes.

* Melody from Naumann's *History of Music*, where it is transposed a major second lower. Mr. Naumann, in page 140, tells us:—"The rhythm of the following ode has been arranged by Westphal." And further, in a footnote:—"We have it on no less an authority than Böckh that the above melody was composed by Pindar."

EXAMPLE CXXVIII.

SVAHDEBNO-SHOOTOCПNAHYAH, OR MERRY NUPTIAL SONG, OF NIZHEGOROD,[*] FOR FOUR VOICES.

Not very fast (ney ochen skoro).   (*Repeated in Four Stanzas.*)

[*] *Balakireff*, No. 17. Transposed a major sixth higher.

213. Example CXXVI. is very simple, and very pure. Like the previous Greek song, Example CXII., it makes no scruple at changing the rhythm of the measure whenever effect demands it. Changes of rhythm, it may be mentioned, are very frequent in Oriental music, and, though not a specialty thereof, give to it no small measure of its peculiar charm. The scale of this song consists only of the fundamental major fifth, a fair proof of its venerableness.

EXAMPLE CXXIX.

214. Example CXXVII. boasts a slightly larger compass, descending one note below the limit of the last example, thus:—

EXAMPLE CXXX.

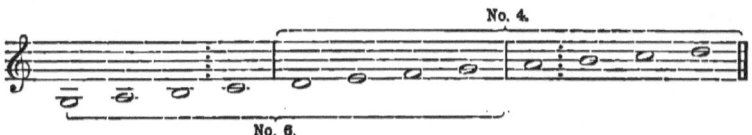

It thus contains that last example's five lower diatonic notes, and the five upper notes of the plagal mode, which also make a major fifth. The claim of both modes being seemingly equal, we give the preference to the parent mode, which, as before mentioned, is not disqualified because of one external note. The present example is professedly the oldest piece of melody in existence, and carries us back to the pre-Christian Greek civilisation, long anterior to the Byzantine epoch. If Mr. Böckh's surmise as to its authorship by Pindar be correct, we have, in this example, a most important contribution to art-history of which it is impossible to over-estimate the value. The naturalness and simplicity, yet withal nobility, of the melody are at once obvious, and we hope are not otherwise than assisted by the moving accompaniment we have constructed for it within the lines of its mode. Mr. Westphal's *rhythmic* arrangement of the ode may be open to question here and there, but, as it is far easier to detect weaknesses than to cure them, we content ourselves with raising the question for the consideration of those who come after, and leave the rhythm as arranged by him.

215. Example CXXVIII. has the same compass as Example CXXVII. and, like Examples CXII. and CXXVI., changes the rhythm occasionally. Its commencement on the fourth of the scale is an old feature to which we shall soon become accustomed. It will be observed that the first portion of the second half of the example is an agreeable variant of the three measures at the commencement.

216.—THE HYPOPHRYGIAN MODE, OR PLAGAL TONE II.

This mode is the same as the Gregorian Mixolydian mode, or Tone 7, and is a favourite with writers of both classes of Music, religious and secular. It is the mode in which the second of the two Chants in Example XVI., and the Choral-dance in Example CVIII.* are respectively written. If we lose in this mode somewhat of the boldness of the parent Phrygian, we part also with some of its hardness and austerity of feature; and its "power of inspiration," if not so exalted, is spread over a larger though perhaps lower level. We give the five following specimens, which, in their way, are each of them excellent.

* *Balakireff*, No. 3. Untransposed.

EXAMPLE CXXXI.
A Parting Song, of Smyrna,* for four voices.
(Repeated in Three Stanzas.)

EXAMPLE CXXXII.
Svahdebnahyah, or Nuptial Song, of Kniaghininski, Nizhegorod,† for four voices.
(Repeated in Seventeen Stanzas.)

* *Ducoudray*, No. 5. Transposed a major fifth higher.   † *Balakireff*, No. 1. Untransposed.

APPLICATION AND SPECIMENS.

EXAMPLE CXXXIII.
TRISAGION, FROM COPTIC LITURGY OF ST. BASIL,[*] FOR FOUR VOICES.
(Complete in One Stanza.)

EXAMPLE CXXXIV.
CHOROVODNAHYAH, OR CHORAL-DANCE, OF STAVROPOL, SAMAHRAH,[†] FOR FOUR VOICES.
(Repeated in Nine Stanzas.)

[*] *Scottish Review*, April, 1890, page 348. Untransposed. † *Balakireff*, No. 5. Transposed a major fourth higher.

EXAMPLE CXXXV.

CHOROVODNAIIYAII, OR CHORAL-DANCE, OF PRAMZEENAII, SIMBIRSK,* FOR FOUR VOICES.

217. Examples CXXXI. and CXXXII. are both framed on the five upper notes of the plagal mode, thus possessing a compass of one note less than Examples CXXVII. and CXXVIII., and consequently they put forth claims to be adjudged as authentic Phrygian. But the unquestionable influence of the subdominant g-natural sets a bar to those claims, and necessitates a settlement in favour of *The Hypophrygian Mode*. That the same notes in the same mode are able to serve the widely differing purposes of "parting" and "nuptials," is a fair indication of the universal adaptability of the mode.

EXAMPLE CXXXVI.

No. 6.

Example CXXXI., like the Examples CXII., CXXVI., and CXXVIII., changes the time, though once only.

218. In Example CXXXIII. we have a fine specimen of ancient Greek ecclesiastical melody, which is unmistakably pre-Dioscorian, and which we have elsewhere † described as "perfect in form, and perfect in matter." It occupies the lower trichord of each of the two Phrygian tetrachords of scale No. 4, in inverse order, which six notes beautifully balance themselves in the Hypophrygian scale, No. 6, as did the six Dorian notes of Example CXVIII. in the Hypodorian mode, thus :—

EXAMPLE CXXXVII.

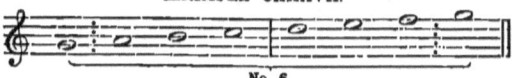

No. 6.

* *Balakireff*, No. 22. Transposed a major second higher. † *Scottish Review*, April 1800, page 347.

APPLICATION AND SPECIMENS. 99

219. Example CXXXIV. is the same in melody with Example CXXI. Referring back to that example, we find that the scale of the melody corresponded to the authentic Dorian mode, while the dependance of that melody upon the subdominant of the mode marked its plagal character as Hypodorian, in which mode it was accordingly harmonised. But the anomaly of a plagal melody being confined to the octave limit of the authentic scale gives rise to the suspicion that there is something wrong somewhere. Reviewing the scale upon which the melody is framed, at Example CXXV., we notice that the second lowest note of the scale is non-existent. That note is f-natural. This is the clue to the mystery. In the process of formation of the scale in the infancy of the art, certain notes were later than others in asserting themselves, and obtaining recognition. Hundreds of ancient melodies in all countries bear witness to this fact by being minus those notes. But f-natural is never one of those missing notes. In fact it is one of the first existent notes, and forms part of even the briefest of known scales.

220. Let us for a few moments turn our thoughts to the principle of transposition. Generally, if we desire to elevate or depress a melody in a natural scale, we have recourse to the modulating or transposing characters, sharps and flats. Thus, to raise a melody one tone, we add two sharps; to lower it a tone, we add two flats. To raise it two tones, we add four sharps; to lower it two tones, we add four flats, and so on. But if the melody chance to be of very small compass, of two, three, four, five, or six notes only, we are not of necessity obliged to use transposing characters. Thus, the melody of Examples CIX. and CX. might equally well occupy the upper tetrachord of Example CXIV.; Example CXXVI. might occupy the upper tetrachord of Example CXXIX., with one additional note (e); Examples CXXVII. and CXXVIII. might occupy the five upper notes of Example CXXX., with one additional note (e); and Examples CXXXI. and CXXXII. might occupy the five lower notes of Example CXXXVI., without in any one case requiring a sharp or flat to assist the transposition. Now let us take the notes of the scale in Example CXXV., and transpose them a major fifth lower, thus:—

EXAMPLE CXXXVIII.
No. 4.
No. 6.

and we see that the missing note is no longer f-natural, but b-natural. B-natural was, historically and constructively, the last note added to the diatonic scale. The fact of b-natural being the missing note in this melody helps to determine the question of its mode, which is made more certain by its plagal commencement and tonal final combinedly securing for it a position as a member of the Hypophrygian family rather than the Hypodorian. Example CXXI., like Example CXX., had a plagal fourth commencement and plagal final, which, as good Hypodorian marks, gave great colour to the usurpation which we have now endeavoured to overthrow.

221. It will be seen that the normal setting in Example CXXXIV. is very low in compass, and would be better for performance if raised a major fifth, as in Example CXXI. But the question here arises:—whether, if a melody be placed in another than its normal mode, it should be harmonised in that new mode, or should carry its normal harmony with it? Of course this question can only arise when a melody is transposable without sharps or flats, as in the present and the seven other instances above referred to. The question is an open one: in the Church it is wisely discountenanced, as we urged in paragraph 48; in secular music a little more latitude is claimed; and as the present melody was one of the best instances that could offer for illustration, we decided to insert it, while the matter was *sub judice*, at Example CXXI., in the harmony of the new mode to which it was transferred, to show the great change of character which can be effected by a new harmonic dress. And to make the change more obvious, we now submit the normal harmony of Example CXXXIV. transposed after the ordinary fashion, and placed at the altitudinal level of Example CXXI.

o 2

EXAMPLE CXXXIX.

TRANSPOSED VERSION OF EXAMPLE CXXXIV.*

(*Repeated in Nine Stanzas.*)

We beg the reader to notice the difference in effect of the Hypodorian f-natural in the accompanying parts of Example CXXI. and the Hypophrygian b-natural in the accompanying parts of Example CXXXIV., which latter note is now transposed into f-sharp.

222. Example CXXXV., like Example CXXXIV., also lacks the b-natural. But it involves a greater series of notes, extending to a minor tenth, than any of the previous examples. Its compass covers a minor seventh of the authentic scale, equally with a minor seventh of the plagal scale, thus:—

EXAMPLE CXL.

in this respect exceeding the compass of Example CXXXIV. as displayed in Example CXXXVIII., which gave us only an authentic major fifth against a plagal minor seventh. The freedom and liveliness of the present Choral-dance is patent to all. The commencement, like that of Example CXX., is on the plagal fourth, or seventh authentic.

223. THE LYDIAN MODE, OR TONE III.

This, the best known to modern musicians of all the modes as the Major mode, the mode in which the transposed tune "Newtown" in Example XVII. is composed, answers to the Gregorian Hypolydian mode, or Tone 6. It has always been a favourite with secular composers, though fought shy of for many centuries by churchmen. The epithet applied to it by the latter of "The Wanton Mode" may be deemed just or otherwise according to individual predilection. Because of its present general use, we need give none other than the following instance.

* *Balakireff*, No. 5. Transposed a minor second lower.

EXAMPLE CXLI.
An Exile's Song, of Smyrna.*
(Complete in Two Stanzas.)

* *Ducoudray*, No. 7. Transposed a minor fourth higher.

102   BYZANTINE MUSIC.

224. The poet Dryden may be almost imagined to have had Example CXLI. in mind, when he penned his well-known distich—

"Softly sweet, in Lydian measure,
Soon he sooth'd his soul to pleasure."

The melody is formed of the lower six notes of the authentic scale, and is singularly chaste and beautiful.

EXAMPLE CXLII.
No. 9.

225. THE HYPOLYDIAN MODE, OR PLAGAL TONE III., COMMONLY CALLED THE BARYTONE.*

This mode agrees with the Gregorian Lydian mode, or Tone 5. It is the mode in which the transposed tune "Old Hundredth" in Example XVII. is composed. It is the sharpest in effect of all the "major keys," as before mentioned in paragraph 24, having each interval of the scale major, thus:—

EXAMPLE CXLIII.
HYPOLYDIAN MODE.   ALL MAJOR INTERVALS.

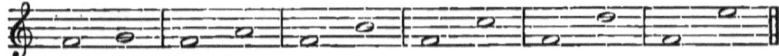

226. Melodies in this, as in each of the plagal modes, are near akin to those in the parent authentic mode, though lower in pitch. Consequently, in this mode, they are, to the modern mind, all as one with melodies in the Lydian mode, and are equally styled "in the major key." As it was difficult to choose between the merits of the three following examples, each is inserted.

EXAMPLE CXLIV.
BOORLATSKAHYAH, OR BOATMEN'S SONG,† OF TAMBOFF.‡

* Or Heavy-tone, being the lowest in pitch of *The Oriental Natural Diatonic Series*, and bearing the alone major fourth. See note, p. 23.
† See also Example CXIX. The workmen on the river boats of the Volga and its tributaries are styled *Boorlahky*, which term assimilates them to the English class of boatmen styled *Bargees*.   ‡ *Balakireff*, No. 13. Transposed a minor sixth higher.

APPLICATION AND SPECIMENS. 103

EXAMPLE CXLV.

CHOROVODNAIIYAH, OR CHORAL-DANCE, OF ASTRAKHAN,† FOR FOUR VOICES.

Moderately (oomeyrcuno). (*Repeated in Twenty Stanzas.*)

* The present, together with Example CVIII., having no pause until the conclusion of the last stanza, are practically "Continuous-songs" equally with Example CXX., though minus the characteristic *codetta*. See paragraph 210.

† *Balakireff*, No. 20. Transposed a minor fifth higher. This instance of fivefold or quintuple measure is accentuated differently to what Western musicians are accustomed to. In the *Allegretto* movement of the Cavatine "Viens, gentille Dame" in Boieldieu's Opera *La Dame Blanche*, and in the final movement of Reeve's *Gipsies' Glee* "Oh, who has seen the miller's wife?" the triple-time member of the measure precedes the common-time member, so that the bars stand thus,—1, 2, 3 : 1, 2. Mr. Reeve has

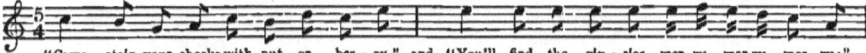

"Come, stain your cheeks with nut or ber‑ry," and "You'll find the gip‑sies mer‑ry, mer‑ry, mer‑ry;"

and this giving of precedence to the numerically greater member of the measure is justified by those who defend it, not on account of any peculiarity in the rhythm of the words, which would be a good defence so far as it can carry, but upon what is thought to be a parallel instance in the sevenfold or septuple measure, where the numerically greater member takes the lead, thus,—1, 2, 3, 4 : 1, 2, 3. But we submit, with all respect, that the fourfold member of the septuple measure precedes the triplet because of the greater perfection of the common-time, not on account of the greater number of beats. The same cause has induced the above Example CXLV. to give precedence to the common-time though smaller member of the measure, thus,—1, 2, : 1, 2, 3.

104 BYZANTINE MUSIC.

EXAMPLE CXLVI.
A SAILOR'S LOVE SONG, OF LEUCADIA.*
(Repeated in Four Stanzas.)

Moderato.

Κα - ρά - βιν' ἔυ' ἀ - πὸ τὴ Χιό, Μὲ τοὺς βαρ-κού-λαις του ταῖς

Poco riten.

δυό, 'Στὴν ἄμ-μον πῆ - γε κι ἄ - ρα - ξε, Κά - θι - σε καὶ λο - γά - ρια - σε.

227. These three examples are each of the same compass of a major ninth, of which six notes are authentic, while seven are plagal, thus determining the mode.

EXAMPLE CXLVII.

No. 9.

No. 12.

228. Example CXLIV. is a very robust specimen of the Russian *Barcarole*. It differs considerably from its precursor at Example CXIX., and, like Examples CXXXIV. and CXXXV., is minus the b-natural.

229. Example CXLV. is the first instance we have had of quintuplo time, a measure of which Eastern peoples are very fond. There is nothing forced or unnatural in the application of the measure in this example, but the change to triple time will, no doubt, be very welcome.

230. Example CXLVI. is a marked and distinctive melody originating with the Leucadians, but now well known in all parts of Greece. It has a "jolly tar" kind of swing with it, which never fails to give pleasure.

231. The only remaining note of the natural diatonic scale to serve as a tonic is b-natural, which furnishes us with the least perfect of all the modes, the Mixolydian Mode, which possesses the top-heavy tritonal tetrachord of variety 1 in paragraph 40.

232. THE MIXOLYDIAN MODE, OR TONE IV.,

Agrees with the Gregorian Hypophrygian mode, or Tone 4. This, the exact opposite of the Hypolydian mode, is the most depressed of all the "minor keys," having each interval of the scale minor, thus :—

* *Ducoudray*, No 25. On the authority of Mr. Skiadaressi, of Athens. Transposed a major third higher.

EXAMPLE CXLVIII.
MIXOLYDIAN MODE. ALL MINOR INTERVALS.

233. But to point more distinctly the contrast between the two modes, we bring together the Examples CXLIII. and CXLVIII., of the Hypolydian and Mixolydian modes respectively, and reduce them to a common octave, thus:—

EXAMPLE CXLIX.
1. MAJOR INTERVALS. Common Octave.

2. MINOR INTERVALS. Common Octave.

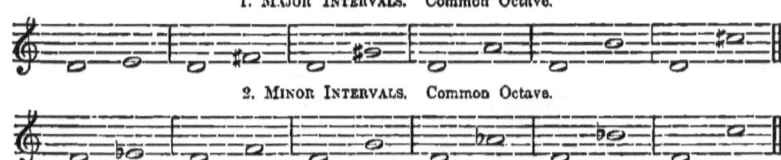

234. Here we see that the former requires the ordinary first three sharps, ƒ, c, and g, and the latter the ordinary first three flats, B, E, and A.

235. On account of the fifth of the Mixolydian scale being minor, it is held by harmonists that the tonic is unable to serve as a ground or foundation note, as it cannot sustain a final harmony. That final harmony can command a major fifth in all other modes, and has need to perfect its effect by sharpening only the third in the minor modes of e-natural, a-natural, and d-natural. But in the present mode of b-natural there would be need to sharpen the fifth also as well as the third; and this would either make the mode a mere transposition, or give to its tonic a character foreign to the scale. Consequently the tonic in this mode is always treated harmonically as a major third of its sub-mediant, g-natural. This by no means confuses the Mixolydian with the Hypophrygian, the fundamental note of the latter being the major fifth, d-natural, instead of the major third, b-natural.

236. In paragraph 220 we mention the fact that melodies of small compass may be transposed without the modulating characters sharps and flats. Consequently such melodies may be thought to be natural to two modes though such is not really the case. But it requires close attention, and sometimes a nice balancing of probabilities, to judge which is the true mode of those very convenient melodies. Two of the cases referred to of this facile transposition were Examples CIX. and CX. These examples were framed upon the lower or fundamental tetrachord of scale No. 1, the Dorian mode, as in Example CXIV. But the two tetrachords of scale No. 1, being similar in form, Examples CIX. and CX. would lie equally well upon the upper tetrachord of that scale. But it is unusual to place a melody at the upper part of an authentic scale to the exclusion of the lower part, though it is common enough to do so at the upper part of plagal scales, as we have already sufficiently proved. The upper tetrachord of the Dorian mode must then, in a case of transposition such as we are now considering, be made to occupy a fundamental position, and this it does in scale No. 13, the Mixolydian mode, thus:—

EXAMPLE CL.
No. 13.

on the lower tetrachord of which our second instances of Examples CIX. and CX., are respectively based.

106 BYZANTINE MUSIC.

EXAMPLE CLI.
LESSER INTROIT, FROM SUNDAY LITURGY OF THE RUSSIAN CHURCH, FOR FOUR VOICES.
(Complete in One Stanza.)

EXAMPLE CLII.
ALLELUIA OF THE APOSTLE, FROM LITURGY OF THE RUSSIAN CHURCH, FOR FOUR VOICES.
(Complete in One Stanza.)

APPLICATION AND SPECIMENS.   107

237. The melody in both these examples is unquestionably Dorian rather than Mixolydian, the Dorian mode taking precedence of the Mixolydian, (1) in date of formation; (2) in fundamentability of form; and (3) in order of number. But although the melodies are in theory Dorian, they are practically treated in Russia as Mixolydian by musicians of the modern school: hence the necessity for reprinting them in their present form. Two Russian peculiarities are also retained in the present form: (1) the extra penultimate note in Example CLI.; and (2) the unscholastic sequence of thirds with the melody in Example CLII. It is worthy of remark that the two examples with which we commenced THE NATURAL DIATONIC SERIES (forming CLASS 1 of Example LXXI.) also close the Series.

238. THE ARTIFICIAL DIATONIC SERIES, A. and B., consisting of those scales formed from the diatonic tetrachords which need for their normal signatural definition one and two sharps, or one and two flats, next claim our attention. These Series constitute CLASSES 2 and 3 in Examples LXXIII. and LXXV. It is not very easy to discover an entire melody written in any one of these modes. Fragments may be found in abundance, springing from, or leading to, other modes; but entire melodies are scarce.

239. SERIES A.

This is the Series whose parent scale, No. 8, corresponds to the at one time commonly received ascending form of the minor mode, with a major sixth and a major seventh. The series is tabulated in part at Example XXV., and in full, as CLASS 2, at Example LXXIII. We give two instances in illustration thereof: the one partial, the other complete.

EXAMPLE CLIII.
A LOVER'S SONG, OF SMYRNA.*
(*Complete in Two Stanzas.*)

* *Ducoudray*, No. 18. Untransposed.

EXAMPLE CLIV.
An Adulatory Song, of Smyrna.*
(*Complete in Two Stanzas.*)

* Ducoudray, No. 21. Untransposed.

APPLICATION AND SPECIMENS.   109

240. Example CLIII. is formed of two distinct scales: the first being the Hypolydiophrygian of the present Series at Example XXV., which forms a *Pseudo-Hypophrygian Mode*, A.*; the second being the Mixolydian of the *natural* diatonic series at Example XXIV.

EXAMPLE CLV.

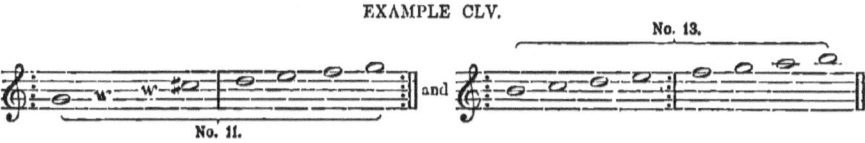

Notice must be taken that the first three bars or measures of Example CLIII. require every *c* to be sharpened. In the second and third bars the diminished tetrachord No. 12 (*c d e f*), characteristic of this Series, is especially observable. C-natural prevails in each of the following bars. The second portion of the melody is a good secular instance of the mode last treated of in the *natural* diatonic series.

241. Example CLIV., though beyond the pale of the scales exhibited in Example XXV., finds full recognition in Example LXXIII., Nos. 125 and 136. Its characteristic diminished tetrachord common to both scales, though foreign to the *natural* diatonic series, is, as above mentioned, proper to the present *artificial* series, being formed upon the major seventh of the parent scale. The melody may be fitly described as of *The Pseudo-Hypomixolydian Mode*, A.†

EXAMPLE CLVI.

Being without change of mode, Example CLIV. is a very interesting specimen of the series. The Hypomixolydian mode was not recognised in the *natural* diatonic series, being identical with the Dorian mode. In the present *artificial* series the two modes are not identical, the *Pseudo-Dorian* (Phrygiodorian), No. 3, having e-natural as its limits, the *Pseudo-Hypomixolydian*, No. 136, having e-flat. It will be observed that E is flattened throughout Example CLIV. without any exception. The quintuple measure also cannot fail to strike the reader, as the present is a particularly happy instance thereof, divided accentually after the manner of Example CXLV.

242. While in the *natural* diatonic Series the transposing sharps (from left to right) and flats (from right to left) follow the well-known order from the normal blank in the centre:—

F	C	G	D	A	E	B	—	*f*	*c*	*g*	*d*	*a*	*e*	*b*
C	G	D	A	E	B				*f*	*c*	*g*	*d*	*a*	*e*
G	D	A	E	B						*f*	*c*	*g*	*d*	*a*
D	A	E	B								*f*	*c*	*g*	*d*
A	E	B										*f*	*c*	*g*
E	B												*f*	*c*
B														*f*

* This is styled a Pseudo-Hypophrygian Mode, because another Pseudo-Hypophrygian can be formed in this SERIES A., by using the g-natural scale with e-flat, No. 5; and it is styled a *Pseudo*-Hypophrygian, not only as differing from the true Hypophrygian scale, No. 6, but also because the alternative scales of Nos. 11 and 5 may with equal propriety claim to be a Pseudo-Hypolydian Mode, A., on f-natural, and a Pseudo-Hypodorian Mode, A., on a-natural respectively.

† This being the only possible instance in SERIES A., it is styled *the* Pseudo-Hypomixolydian Mode.

110   BYZANTINE MUSIC.

In the present *artificial* Series A. they follow another order from the two normal signatures c and E with an intervening instance of a flat and sharp combined, thus:—

F	C	G	D	A	E	D ♭	c	g	d	a	e	b
C	D	A	E	B			f	c	g	d	a	
D	A	E	B					f	c	g	d	
A	E	B							f	c	g	
E	B									f	c	
B											f	

243. SERIES B.

Series B, of the Oriental ARTIFICIAL DIATONIC scales, tabulated in part at Example XXVI., and in full as CLASS 3, at Example LXXV., differs from Series A. in possessing two diminished fourth tetrachords within its limits, both of which are of the diatonic genus, in place of one such tetrachord only, the which one diminished fourth tetrachord of Series A. is really an anticipation of the chromatic genus. The peculiarity of the scales in Series B. consists, as before pointed out, in the five tones and two semitones, of which every diatonic scale is formed, being each undivided. This throwing together of five tones in succession gives an air of intense sharpness in the ascending scale, and of corresponding depression in the descending scale. But the junction of the two semitones is the most index-like feature, and compels immediate attention. We alluded earlier in this work to a well-known modern instance of this concurrence of the two semitones,—that of the e-flat in a D minor passage in the first figure of the original *Lancer's Quadrille*. This passage we here transpose a major second lower, into C minor, in order to place the Lydiodorian phrase at the close in one of its normal positions, that with flats.

EXAMPLE CLVII.

244. It will be seen that this Example CLVII. is a mere fragment, and with such fragments, longer certainly in some cases, we are, generally, at present, obliged to be content. But to show the thorough adaptability of the scales of this series for melodic purposes, we have composed a short *Aria*, of two sections of four measures each, in the normal parent mode of the Series with sharps, the second section of which, having a complete scale passage, may almost suggest to the student a practicable and proper *Rule of the Octave*. The two sharps to be borne in mind in performance are c and d.

EXAMPLE CLVIII.

ARIA PATETICA, IN SLOW DANCE MEASURE, FOR THE PIANOFORTE.

Andantino moderato.   (*To be repeated ad libitum.*)

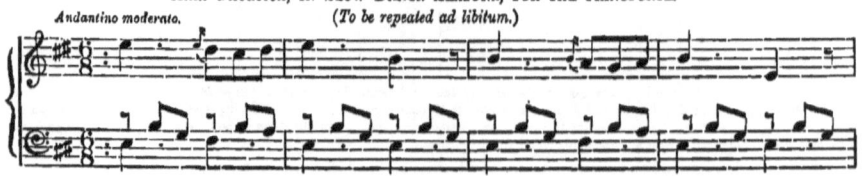

APPLICATION AND SPECIMENS. 111

245. This Example CLVIII. occupies the whole of the Lydiodorian scale, which may be styled *The Pseudo-Dorian Mode*, B.,* of Example XXVI., and the leading note below, thus :—

EXAMPLE CLIX.
No. 7.

The extra note beyond the octave scale does not incapacitate the melody from being affiliated to that scale, while the presence of that extra note in this example furnishes an apt illustration of the peculiarity of Series B., by giving, at the lower part of the example, the two semitones in juxtaposition, from d-sharp to f-natural, followed by the group of five tones from the same f-natural to the d-sharp above. We commend the scales of this Series to the attention of our readers. There are possibilities within reach in connection therewith not yet dreamed of.

246. The order of the sharps and flats in transposing the scales of this artificial diatonic Series B., from the two normal signatures c d and E D, with three intervening instances of both characters combined, is as follows :—

F	C	G	D	A	*f*	E	*c*	B	*g*	*d*	*a*	*e*	*b*
G	D	A	E	B					*f*	*c*	*g*	*d*	*a*
A	E	B								*f*	*c*	*g*
E	B										*f*	*c*
B												*f*

247. We approach now THE PURE CHROMATIC SERIES, which will be found tabulated in full as CLASS 4, at Example LXXVII. Its double share of minor second semitonal intervals as compared with the three Series of diatonic scales, and the presence of two instances of the augmented second interval, give all its scales, and the Oriental music based upon them, that peculiarly weird character remarked by all travellers in the East.

248. We have singled out four specimen examples which admit no admixture of other scales, and which, though perhaps not so taking as some of the more mixed specimens later on, claim a great pre-eminence in the matter of purity. The first example is a small Dance-tune introduced by the Armenian composer Mr. D. Tchouhadjian in his clever Turkish Opera *Leblebidji Hor-hor Agha* (Stamboule [Constantinople]: H. Aramian & Cie.); the three others are popular Turkish songs selected from Signor Callisto Guatelli's *Album : 24 Arie nazionali e Canti popolari Orientali, antichi e moderni* (Constantinopoli: F. H. Schimpff & Cie.). These latter are old undated specimens, and, although usually denominated Turkish, even by Greeks, are undoubtedly Greek in their origin. The Turks, respectfully though we may regard them as individuals, are not as a nation artistic. In the fourteenth and fifteenth centuries, when they

* This is the only unambiguous instance of the Pseudo-Dorian Mode in SERIES B., the e-flat form of scale No. 24 being more truly the Pseudo-Hypomixolydian Mode, B.; and the alternative scale of No. 7 in Example CLVII. may with equal propriety claim to be the Pseudo-Lydian Mode, B., on e-natural.

112   BYZANTINE MUSIC.

over-ran the civilised lands constituting the Byzantine empire, they not only possessed no Architecture or Music of their own, but they saw at once that there was no need of their possessing any, both being made ready to their hand in the countries conquered by them. Hence Turkish Architecture and Turkish Music when not spoiled by foreign admixture are both of them essentially Greek, or, more distinctively, Byzantine. We call the reader's attention to the two sharps, *g* and *d*, of the first and third examples; and the two flats, A and D, of the second and fourth.

EXAMPLE CLX.
ORIENTAL DANCE, FOR THE PIANOFORTE.

EXAMPLE CLXI.
TURKISH SCHIARKY,* FOR THE PIANOFORTE.

* *Guntelli*, Series II., No. 8. In the normal mode with sharps, a major third higher.

APPLICATION AND SPECIMENS.

114 BYZANTINE MUSIC.

EXAMPLE CLXII.
TURKISH SCHARKY,* FOR THE PIANOFORTE.

* *Guatelli*, Series I., No. 9.   † Transposed a minor fourth higher.

APPLICATION AND SPECIMENS.

‡ An octave higher.

EXAMPLE CLXIII.

Turkish Schiarky,* for the Pianoforte.

* *Guatelli*, Series II., No. 4.   † Transposed a major second higher.   ‡ Transposed a major fifth higher.   § Transposed a major ninth higher.

APPLICATION AND SPECIMENS. 117

249. After the experience of Example CLX., we think few readers will vote the Byzantine Chromatic genus to be of necessity dull. The melodic rhythm of this example is perfect, each of the two periods of eight measures consisting of two similar sections formed of two phrases of two measures each. There is a delightful vagueness caused by the absence of the interval of the third from the first two accompanying left hand measures (as also from the fifth and sixth); and this is one secret of the harmonic charm of Oriental music. The melody lies fairly well within the influence of the normal Chromatic scale, No. 49, exceeding its limits by one note each above and below.

EXAMPLE CLXIV.
No. 49.

250. Example CLXI. is of another and sterner character. Its compass of ten notes is a semitone greater in extent to that of Example CLX., and differs much from it in scale position.

EXAMPLE CLXV.
No. 49.

No. 88.

It lies less in the authentic mode, No. 49 (six notes), than in its plagal, No. 88, of which it occupies the whole. But taking the example period by period, we find the authentic and the plagal modes each fairly represented. Thus, periods 1 and 5 are authentic, exceeding its limit by one note only, the leading note below. Period 6 is as clearly plagal, taking an additional note only, the note above. Periods 2 and 3 take in the whole of the ten notes occupied, which being eight to the plagal as against six to the authentic, make it that they carry the day for the plagal mode. Period 4 is a duplication of period 2.

251. Example CLXII. is rather a rhythmical paradox. Its three periods are of the abnormal length of ten, ten, and twelve measures. The two tens can be reconciled to rule by regarding the first two measures of each as premonitory or invitatory. The remaining eight bars of each then fall into position, and divide up into sections and phrases. But the period of twelve bars is a difficulty. The long duplicated section of four and a half measures ending with the triplets, occupies different positions in the two halves of the period: reaching forward to fill the last bar of the first half, and reaching backward to commence its first half measure in the first bar of the second half, thus leaving place in the last bar for the final note. There is no accounting for this. It is far easier to describe the anomaly than to justify it. The almost continuous drone of the accompaniment is a special feature of this example, and very noteworthy. The melodic compass is nearly similar to that in Example CLXIV., minus the additional note above, making a range of nine notes only.

EXAMPLE CLXVI.
No. 49.

252. In the East it is not unusual, when the notes become inconveniently high or inconveniently low to suit his voice, for a singer to modulate into another key,* as we should style it, taking his mode, whatever it may be, with

* For the matter of that, instrumentalists do the same, as, e.g., our present Signor Guatelli. But effect, not convenience, is the constraining motive in their case.

him. It is a pure transposition of a portion of the music. If the reader will refer to signs † and ‡ in Example CLXII., he will see that, presuming the first key to be the standard, there are three transpositions out of it and back again, in all six changes. These changes in the instrumental version by Sig. Guatelli are a fair representation of what the vocalist more frequently does than not, and we think it well to reproduce a specimen of this transposition upon a transposition, to show by contrast with our normal examples what changes of effect are brought about by this double process. But we will first give the order of the sharps and flats in transposing the scales of the pure chromatic series from the two normal signatures *g d* and A D, with three intervening instances of both characters combined.

F	C	G	D	A *f*	E *c*	B *g*	*d*	*a*	*e*	*b*
C	G	D	A	E	D *f*	*c*	*g*	*d*	*a*	*e*
A	E	B						*f*	*c*	*g*
E	B								*f*	*c*
B										*f*

EXAMPLE CLXVII.
Transposed Melody of Example CLXII.*

We have left the reader to supply the transposed harmonies in the above from the model at Example CLXII.

* Literal transcription of *Guatelli*, Series I., No. 8.

APPLICATION AND SPECIMENS. 119

253. The melody of Example CLXIII. extends over a compass of fourteen notes, thus:—

EXAMPLE CLXVIII.

so that it reaches from a semitone below the normal authentic mode to a semitone above the hyper plagal mode. But it is the first period only which is thus extreme: it alone occupies thirteen out of the fourteen notes. The other two periods occupy only the normal authentic octave with the semitone below. The reader is recommended to transpose the present example agreeably to the footnotes, after the manner of Example CLXVII., supplying, as before, the transposed harmonies.

254. We now present to notice three specimens based each on two modes, the pure chromatic and the natural diatonic. We are glad to be able to revert in two of the instances to Greek words. The whole of the so-called Turkish songs no doubt once possessed Greek words, but we have only been fortunate enough to discover a few. The Turkish words, were we to insert them, would be of small utility except to those who read Arabic characters; but Arabic, Persian, and Turkish readers would give us small thanks were we to insert them, because the musical notation, reading from left to right, would involve a syllabic inversion of the words far more difficult to decipher than a literal inversion. It would appear to their eyes like the two headlines on the two present open pages, if printed thus, would appear to us:—

| 119 | MENSCISPE AND TIONCAPLIAP. | | SICMU TINEZANBY. | 118 |

255. Our first instance is a very perfect example: the once-occurring appogiatural euphonic g-natural in bar 7 in no way damaging its claims to purity. The signatural sharps are *g* and *d*.

EXAMPLE CLXIX.

AN ANXIOUS-LOVER'S SONG, OF ATHENS.*

(*Repeated in Three Stanzas.*)

* *Ducoudray*, No. 29. On the authority of Mr. Gérojannis, of Athens. Transposed a major second higher.

APPLICATION AND SPECIMENS.   121

256. Thus pure and perfect, it would have found its place with the previous four examples, but for the fact that M. Ducoudray gives, with a repetition of the last two lines of the stanza, a Coda written in the natural diatonic genus, as follows:—

EXAMPLE CLXX.

Coda of Example CLXIX.

This diatonic Coda is, as a portion of the melody, an anachronism. It has, no doubt, long existed, but is of subsequent date to the completed chromatic melody, and most probably originated in the desire of some instrumental accompanist to interpose a few notes between the stanzas for the relief of the singer. In process of time, these added notes got to be regarded as part of the tune, and at length some popular singer ventured to utilise them, repeating for the purpose the last two lines of each stanza. A parallel instance, of this hardening of a fancy till it becomes to all appearance an undoubted fact, has occurred in the writer's own experience. The peal of bells in the tower of St. Mary Redcliffe Church, Bristol, was supplied (we think some time in the last century) with a chiming barrel on which was set the Old 113th Psalm tune, consisting of twelve strains of eight notes each, which tune is given four times, at each of the hours of I., V., and IX., day and night. But the artist engaged in setting the tune, finding he had at the end thereof a little space left on the barrel, which, if unoccupied, would leave a gap of silence between the four stanzas whenever the chimes sounded, struck upon the happy thought of filling the space with the descending Lydian scale No. 9, which scale of eight notes paves the way admirably for the next stanza. This was proper as regards the artist and his dilemma. But the effect upon generations of listeners to those chimes has been to make them believe that the added thirteenth strain of eight notes is part and parcel of the original tune. It was years before the writer could disabuse himself of this false impression, and when at last he knew better and succeeded in doing so, he found others quite as obstinate in defence of these added notes as he himself had been. Just in the same way, most probably, has Example CLXX. grown up to be, in the estimation of many Easterns, an integral portion of Example CLXIX. As an interlude between the stanzas, its presence in a different mode is somewhat misleading, though, as we will immediately prove, such misleading passages are in common enough use.

257. Our next example is an instance of the principle of the previous paragraph applied in the contrary way, where a diatonic song has a chromatic interlude, which is made to serve also as a Prelude to the first stanza. The prelude only has sharps g and d.

R

EXAMPLE CLXXI.
Turkish Schiarky,* for the Pianoforte.

* From a Constantinople MS. Also in *Guatelli*, Series I., No. 2. † Transposed a major second higher.

APPLICATION AND SPECIMENS.   123

258. Our next example is, as all previous extracts from M. Ducoudray have been, excepting Example CLXIX., without any doubtful extraneous adjuncts.

EXAMPLE CLXXII.
A NAUTICAL SONG, OF SMYRNA.*
(Complete in Two Stanzas.)

* *Ducoudray*, No. 10. Transposed a minor fourth higher.

124   BYZANTINE MUSIC.

259. Example CLXIX. covers a compass of eleven notes, from the leading note below the plagal No. 88 of the normal chromatic mode, to the minor sixth of the authentic, No. 49. Example CLXX. occupies a still wider range of twelve notes, from the lowest note of *The Hypodorian Mode*, No. 2, to the highest note of the parent *Dorian*, No. 1.

EXAMPLE CLXXIII.

But taking Example CLXIX. section by section of four measures each, into which the melody, excepting in the final period, divides itself, we find the first four sections lie on the plagal region with varying compass, from four notes in section 4, to nine notes in section 2; while sections 5 and 6, which are similar one to the other, occupy the six notes of the authentic scale. The final period is irregular in form, and does not lend itself to division, being what is generally styled interwoven: the first note of its second section being identical with the last note of its first section, and joined to, not only without pause, but within the actual limits of, that first section. The second section also is contracted seriously in the penultimate measure. Example CLXX. curiously enough follows the irregular rythmical contractions of the final period of CLXIX., beat for beat: a pretty clear proof, we take it, of the subsequent date assigned to this Coda, and of its being the work of an imitator, notwithstanding its change of mode.

260. Example CLXXI. is, as before mentioned, an instance confirmatory of our theory that the Coda of another mode in Example CLXIX. is a mere instrumental addition. We have here an instrumental Prelude (which played at the end forms also a Coda) in quite another mode from the vocal portion. The prelude is in the plagal *Chromatic Mode*, No. 88, and the song proper is in the two forms, plagal and authentic, Nos. 2 and 1, of *The Dorian Mode*.

EXAMPLE CLXXIV.

261. It is one proof of the wonderful elasticity of the Byzantine music, that transpose portions of it as much as we may or must, the ordinary hearer is quite unconscious of the fact, the change seeming so perfectly consistent. In the present instance the prelude and the three prefatory measures of the vocal portion fit quite as smoothly upon the

remainder (from †) transposed a major second higher, with its necessary f-sharp and c-sharp, as they do upon that remainder when untransposed. We are almost tempted to print the example in its transposed as well as its natural form, but the question of space forbids. The reader, however, is invited to transpose it for himself, with the almost certain result, that although he will not prefer it to the natural form, he will probably claim for it superior brilliancy. The rhythmical division is peculiar. While the chromatic prelude is perfectly regular, in a period of eight measures, the vocal portion divides into two periods of thirteen and twelve measures respectively, with a third period which is simply a variation of the second. We may add that the present example is well known all over the Levant, and is a favourite alike with Arabs, Greeks, and Turks.

262. Example CLXXII. is a short but very sweet specimen, based upon the *Lydian* scale, No. 9, and the lower six notes of the normal *Chromatic* scale, No. 49.

EXAMPLE CLXXV.

Attention is called to the effect of the two cases of unresolved major seventh (b-natural) supported by the harmony of the tonic eleventh. The chromatic mode may be said to be "more honoured in the breach than in the observance," being reserved for the last two measures; and even in these the first d, an ascending note, is treated euphonically as d-natural.

263. THE MIXED CHROMATIC SERIES in the three principal varieties, which we propose now to illustrate, are tabulated in full as CLASSES 5, 6, and 7, at Examples LXXIX., LXXXI., and LXXXIII. They constitute in their most normal form, respectively, *The Chromatic Hypodorian Mode*, No. 44; *The Chromatic Lydian Mode*, No. 45; and *The Chromatic Dorian Mode*, No. 43.

264. CLASS 5.

In this Class we furnish three specimens, each of which requires the signature of *g* sharp

EXAMPLE CLXXVI.

A CRADLE SONG, OF SMYRNA.*
(*Complete in One Stanza.*)

* *Ducoudray*, No. 1. Transposed a major second lower.

APPLICATION AND SPECIMENS.

EXAMPLE CLXXVII.
A Disappointed-Lover's Song, of Smyrna.*
(*Complete in Two Stanzas.*)

EXAMPLE CLXXVIII.
Song (without words) from "Lebledidji Hor-hor Agha," for the Pianoforte.

* *Ducoudray*, No. 17. Transposed a major second lower.

Here the 24 bars of Example CLX. come in.* After which we proceed thus:—

* On the authority of the Pianoforte Editor, Mr. J. Assadour. Both examples are untransposed.

265. Example CLXXVI., in *The Hyper Chromatic Hypodorian Mode,** is one of the most characteristic specimens of Byzantine music. It is familiar to the Oriental ear from the earliest infancy, and the eleven-fold falling cadence from g-sharp through f-natural to c-natural is imitated by the babe from the nurse's lips in every household. The recitative measures, at the first two changes into 4/4 time, are very effective. The sub-dominant rising phrase—d c f a—with which the example commences, is a most common, yet bewitching, feature in this school of melody, and may be heard not only in the nursery, but from the minaret when the muezzin calls the faithful Mussulman to prayer; from the boatman tugging at his oar; from the itinerant musician; from the coffee-house entertainer; and from the Hieropsaltis in the Church's holy services. Were we to say all that we feel while scanning this beautiful Example CLXXVI., we should be accused by the Western stranger of extravagance. But when he has entered into its spirit, and its spirit has entered into him, the accusation will be withdrawn.

266. Example CLXXVII. is a shorter instance of the same mode, and shows us the poor "Disappointed-Lover" still under the influence of his mother's or nurse's musical cadences. Both examples are based on the same *Hyper Chromatic Hypodorian* scale, which is exceeded by one note below, but fallen short of by two notes above.

EXAMPLE CLXXIX.

No. 37.

267. Example CLXXVIII. is from the same Opera from whence our first chromatic specimen, Example CLX., was taken. It will be observed that that first specimen forms part of the present example, and should be inserted in the place indicated, making the whole movement, with its two repeats, consist of eighty measures, in ten regular periods of eight measures each. Its compass is greater than that of any piece we have yet considered, taking in the *Chromatic Hypodorian* scale, and the whole compass of *both* its plagal scales, above and below.

EXAMPLE CLXXX.

No. 44.   No. 33.   No. 37.   With the euphonics

268. Before we proceed to the next three examples based upon two modes, the present Class 5 and the pure chromatic of Class 4, two of which examples specially invite the transposition which we still recommend to our readers, we will give the order of the sharps and flats proper for transposing Class 5, from the two normal signatures g and E A, with two intervening instances of both characters combined.

F	C	G	D	A	E f	B c	g	d	a	e	b
C	G	D	A	E	B		f	c	g	d	
D	A	E	B					f	c	g	
A	E	B							f	c	
E	B									f	
B											

---

* If our readers will refer to Example CVI. they will see two instances of *Hyper Chromatic Hypo* scales, Nos. 37 and 39. In the diatonic genus the conjunction of the terms *Hyper* and *Hypo* would have no meaning, as the one would neutralize the other. Thus a *Hyper Diatonic Hypodorian* would be simply a plain Dorian. But in the chromatic genus it is otherwise. A marked difference will be seen in Example CVI. between the *Chromatic Dorian*, No. 43, and the *Hyper Chromatic Hypodorian*, No. 37. In the former the diatonic tetrachord occupies the fundamental position; in the latter the chromatic tetrachord is the lower. (See, in further explanation, paragraph 196.)

130   BYZANTINE MUSIC.

EXAMPLE CLXXXI.

MELODY OF FATMA SULTANA, DAUGHTER OF THE LATE SULTAN,* FOR THE PIANOFORTE.

Guatelli, Series I., No. 3.   † Transposed a minor seventh higher.   ‡ Transposed a minor third higher.

APPLICATION AND SPECIMENS.   131

EXAMPLE CLXXXII.
A DESPONDING-COMPLAINER'S SONG, OF SMYRNA.*
(Complete in One Stanza.)

* *Ducoudray*, No. 2. Transposed a major second higher. Also as a Turkish "SCHIARKY," in *Guatelli*, Series I., No. 4. Transposed a major fifth higher.

s 2

132 BYZANTINE MUSIC.

EXAMPLE CLXXXIII.
TURKISH SCHIARKY,* FOR THE PIANOFORTE.

* *Guatelli*, Series II., No. 2. † Transposed a major second lower. ‡ Transposed a minor third higher.

APPLICATION AND SPECIMENS.

†† Transposed a major second lower (*g* b only).

134   BYZANTINE MUSIC.

269. Of Example CLXXXI. we should, under any circumstances, speak respectfully, for we hold with Dr. Johnson, that when persons of consideration enter the literary field, they should be cordially welcomed, and not be scared away by relentless criticism. But when more than ordinary merit attaches to their work, which is very frequently the case, there is then no room for delicacy or compliment, for they deserve all the praise they get, and "to have their merit handsomely allowed." Our present Example CLXXXI. is the work of a Princess of the Imperial Ottoman reigning family, who is assuredly a musician both by instinct and education. The melody throughout is finely constructed, is perfectly rhythmical, and withal, judged by an Oriental standard, highly pleasing. It is based upon the hyper plagal scale, No. 37, of *The Chromatic Hypodorian Mode*, and upon the authentic Chromatic scale, No. 49, with one period (the third) based upon the hypo plagal Chromatic scale, No. 88.

EXAMPLE CLXXXIV.

270. Example CLXXXII. is mainly in the pure Chromatic mode, but one section (bars 10 to 13) is in our present Class 5, with the normal two flats, E and A.

EXAMPLE CLXXXV.

This example has the ring of genuine Byzantine mediævalism; and has not, happily, been entirely surrendered by the Greek to the Turk, though the latter is wise enough to utilize it. It is both widely known and thoroughly appreciated by all Eastern peoples.

271. Example CLXXXIII., like Example CLXXXII., is mainly in the pure Chromatic mode; one phrase only, of two bars, at commencement of the last period, being in the mixed Chromatic mode of Class 5. It covers eleven notes of the former, involving both the hypo plagal and authentic scales, Nos. 88 and 49, and seven notes of the latter, in the hyper plagal register, No. 37.

EXAMPLE CLXXXVI.

There is an air of fierceness and vigour about this Example CLXXXIII. which cannot fail to arrest attention.

272. CLASS 6.

In this Class we have need of the signature *c g* or A. Before entering on the consideration of its small contingent of examples we will give its transposing table after the manner of those of the previous classes, from the above two normal signatures, with two intervening bracketed instances.

APPLICATION AND SPECIMENS. 135

F	C	G	D	**A**	E	*f*	*b*	*c*	*g*	*d*	*a*	*e*	*b*
D	A	E	B			*f*		*c*	*g*	*d*	*a*	*e*
A	E	B						*f*	*c*	*g*	*d*
E	B								*f*	*c*	*g*
B										*f*	*c*
											f

273. We submit the following two examples in illustration of this class of the Mixed Chromatic Series:—

EXAMPLE CLXXXVII.

TROPARION, FROM THE APOSTICHA AT VESPERS, ON GOOD FRIDAY, IN THE GREEK CHURCH.*

* From *Anthologia Graeca Carminum Christianorum, adornaverunt* W. CHRIST *et* M. PARANAKIS (Lipsiæ: B. G. Teubneri), pages cxxxvi-vii. Transposed a minor fourth lower.

EXAMPLE CLXXXVIII.
A Parting Song, of Smyrna.*
(Complete in Two Stanzas.)

* Ducoudray, No. 19. Transposed a minor third higher.

APPLICATION AND SPECIMENS.   137

274. We have the authority of the Greek Church for including Example CLXXXVII. as 'Hχος β' under the scale No. 112, which Example CVI. describes as *The Chromatic Phrygian Mode*, the Phrygian tetrachord being in the fundamental position, on the left hand.* Whatever objection may be felt for that mode with its minor fifth, and its transposed tetrachord 11,† or preference for the normal Chromatic Lydian mode, No. 45, to which this example is equally closely related, there is no getting behind the ecclesiastical verdict—'Hχος β', or Tone 2.

EXAMPLE CLXXXIX.
No. 112.

The reader will see that the example occupies the whole of the octave scale, excepting the lowest note. The highest note, d-natural, which would have been external to the normal scale, No. 45, is now, by the ecclesiastical order, enclosed within the octave. This example being originally printed without harmony in our *Scottish Review* article, we prefer to let it so remain in the present work. We call attention to "the subdominant rising phrase" of Example CLXXVI. in bars 7 to 9 of the present example, only the epithet "subdominant" will now not apply to the mode one major second above the normal. It must here be styled—"the mediant rising phrase." The minor fifth (a-flat)‡ it will be observed, is, with the exception of the major sixth (b-natural), the most persistent note in the whole melody. In no single instance is it raised in pitch for euphonic purposes.

275. Example CLXXXVIII. is one note less in compass than Example CLXXXVI., yet we have preferred to part with one of that reduced number, and place it as an external note credited to *The Chromatic Lydian Mode*, No. 45, thus :—

EXAMPLE CXC.
No. 45.

rather than classify it either (1) as a *Chromatic Phrygian*, No. 112; (2) a *Chromatic Pseudo-Dorian*, No. 122; (3) a *Hyper Chromatic Mixolydian*, No. 84; or (4) a *Hyper Chromatic Lydian* (with an external lower note), No. 38, in manner following :—

EXAMPLE CXCI.

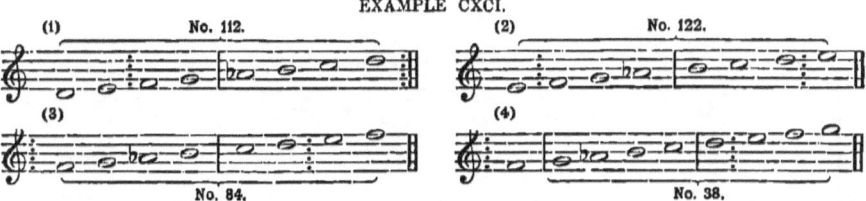

"The subdominant rising phrase" of Example CLXXVI. now falls, in scale No. 45, into its proper order of classification, and is to be found in bars 7 and 10 of Example CLXXXVIII., followed in each instance by the subsequent complete "falling cadence" also. This example, though short, is very perfect.

276. Two examples differing widely in manner, each based upon two modes, the present CLASS 6, and the natural diatonic CLASS 1, now follow :—

* See paragraph 196.   † See paragraphs 197 and 198.   ‡ The remark, at commencement of paragraph 4, as to the "great difference of treatment and effect between" sharps and flats, is well illustrated in the examples of this and the previous Class 5. A-flat is certainly not g-sharp, any more than it is in *Table* at paragraph 18.

T

BYZANTINE MUSIC.

EXAMPLE CXCII.
A Lover's Song, of Smyrna.*
(Complete in Two Stanzas.)

EXAMPLE CXCIII.
An Ardent-Lover's Song, of Smyrna.†
(Complete in Two Stanzas)

* Ducoudray, No. 21. Untransposed.   † Ducoudray, No. 6. Transposed a major fifth higher.

APPLICATION AND SPECIMENS. 139

277. Example CXCII. is mainly written in *The Hyper Chromatic Lydian Mode*, No. 38, with the second note of the chromatic tetrachord sharpened in ascending, after the manner of the similar melodial passage in another tetrachord at close of example CLXXII.

EXAMPLE CXCIV.

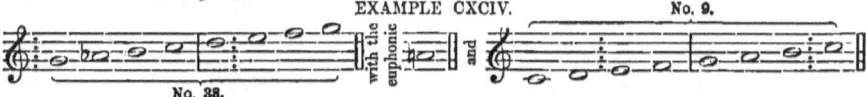

The concluding portion in the diatonic *Lydian Mode* recals, in its phraseology, the salient major seventh effect, based on the harmony of the tonic eleventh, of the same Example CLXXII.

278. Example CXCIII. is also, like Example CLXXII., almost entirely in the diatonic *Lydian Mode*, the chromatic portion being reserved for the last two measures, though the scale of *The Hyper Chromatic Lydian Mode*, No. 38, covers the whole second half of the melody.

EXAMPLE CXCV.

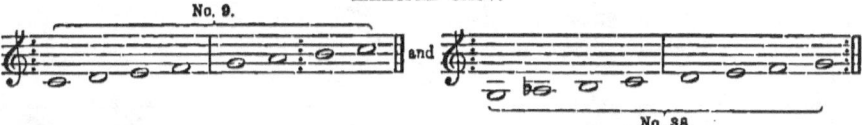

The twofold contracted change in the time is worthy of notice, and the short chromatic cadence at the end has a curious, though telling, effect when given by a rich contralto voice.

T 2

279. Class 7.

This Class requires as its normal signature d or E A D. We give at once its transposing table after the previous manner.

F	C	G	D	A	f	E	c	D	g	d		a	e	b
C	G	D	A	E		D					f	c		g
G	D	A	E	B								f		c
A	E	B												f
E	B													
B														

280. Another Princess of the Turkish Imperial family lays us under obligation for the melody of the mixed example we now furnish.

EXAMPLE CXCVI.

Melody of Geminie Sultana, daughter of the late Sultan,[*] for the Pianoforte.

[*] *Guatelli*, Series I., No. 7. Transposed a major fifth higher.

281. This example is written partly in *The Hyper Chromatic Dorian Mode*, No. 40, proper to Class 7, and in greater part in the authentic and hyper plagal forms of *The Chromatic Lydian Mode*, Nos. 45 and 38, of Class 6.

EXAMPLE CXCVII.

This specimen is scarcely so perfect as its palatial companion and predecessor at Example CLXXXI. Not that it yields thereto in rhythmical correctness, or in general tunefulness, but because its periods, instead of being each in its own mode, change the mode, many of them, during the course of their own individual existence. Thus, dividing the melody into seven periods of eight bars each, while periods 1 and 6 alone comply with the terms of Example CLXXXI., and are wholly in Class 6,

Period 2 contains 3 bars of Class 7, and 5 bars of Class 6;
Period 3 contains 4 bars of Class 7, and 4 bars of Class 6;
Period 4 contains 3 bars of Class 7, and 5 bars of Class 6;
Period 5 contains 2 bars of Class 7, and 6 bars of Class 6;
Period 7 contains 2 bars of Class 7, and 6 bars of Class 6;

giving in all 14 bars, one fourth of the total number, to Class 7, and 42 bars to Class 6. The admixture of these Classes 7 and 6, with their very great dissimilarities, is particularly bold and striking. The concurrence of d-sharp and a-flat, in bar 2 of period 3, is sufficiently pronounced to suit the requirements of the most advanced taste. Yet everything in this connection occurs naturally, and without effort, from the admixture of these two Compound Chromatic Classes, and there is obviously no room or necessity for any kind of caprice. The somewhat ominous phrase at bars 14 to 16 in Example CLXXXVII., is reproduced in semiquavers at bar 8 of periods 1 and 3 in the present example: a plain proof of the Byzantine (we had almost said Ecclesiastical) origin of the so-called Turkish style of music.

282. With this Class 7, the range of the scales formed of the junction of the three diatonic minor fourth tetrachords with the pure chromatic tetrachord, comes to an end. Henceforth, in the remaining eleven classes, with one exception only in Class 8, scale No. 39, *The Hyper Chromatic Hypolydian Mode*, either the diatonic tetrachord is dissonant, or the chromatic tetrachord is off its centre in one of its lateral varieties, or both conditions exist. This makes it convenient to close our classification of examples at this point. But before saying our last word, we will give the transposing table for each of the remaining Classes, in order to lighten the student's labour.

283. CLASS 8. (See Examples LXXXIV.-V.)

F	C	G	D	A	*f*	E	*c*	D	*g*	*d*	*a*	*e*	*b*
A	E	B					*f*		*c*	*g*	*d*	*a*	*e*
C	B							*f*	*c*	*g*	*d*	*a*
B										*f*	*c*
												f

APPLICATION AND SPECIMENS.   143

284. Class 9. (See Examples LXXXVI.-VII.)   **285. Class 10.** (See Examples LXXXVIII.-IX.)

F	C	G	D f	A c	E g	B d	a	e	b
C	G	D	A	E	B			f	c
G	D	A	E	B					f
D	A	E	B						
E	B								
B									

F	C	G	D f	A c	E g	B d	a	e	b
E	D		f		g	d	a	e	
B			f		c	g	d	a	
					f	c	g	d	
						f			c
*									f

286. Class 11. (See Example XC.-I.)   **287. Class 12.** (See Examples XCII.-III.)

F	C	G	D f	A c	E g	B d	a	e	b
G	D	A	E	B f	c	g	d	a	e
E	B			f	c	g	d		
D					f				c
									f

F	C	G	D f	A c	E g	B d	a	e	b
C	G	D	A	E	B f	c	g	d	a
D	A	E	B				f		e
E	D								f
D									

288. Class 13. (See Examples XCIV.-V.)   **289. Class 14.** (See Examples XCVI.-VII.)

F	C	G	D f	A c	E g	B d	a	e	b
G	D	A	E	B			f	c	d
D	A	E	B					f	c
E	B								f
D									

F	C	G	D f	A c	E g	B d	a	e	b
D	A	E	B			f	c	g	d
E	B					f	c	g	d
D							f	c	

290. Class 15. (See Examples XCVIII.-IX.)   **291. Class 16.** (See Examples C.-I.)

F	C	G	D f	A c	E g	B d	a	e	b
C	G	D	A	E f	B c	g	d	a	e
G	D	A	E	B		f			c
E	B								f
D									

F	C	G	D f	A c	E g	B d	a	e	b
C	G	D	A	E f	B c	g	d	a	e
E	B			f	c	g	d	a	
D							f		c
†									f

292. Class 17. (See Examples CII.-III.)   **293. Class 18.** (See Examples CIV.-V.)

E	B f	F c	C g	G d	D a	A e	E b	B F	C
G	D	A	E	B		f		c	d
D	A	E	B					g	d
A	E	B						c	g

E	B f	F c	C g	G d	D a	A e	E b	B F	C
D	A	E	B		f		c	g	d
A	E	D						c	g
							f	c	g

* This being the last Class capable of bearing normally a single signatural sharp or flat, it may be as well to exhibit those single signatures in a short formula, thus:—

Signatures,	a	D	A	E	B	—	f	c	g	d	a
Classes,	10	8	6	4	2		2	5	7	9	

It will be seen that while c-sharp and e-flat are utilised for the two varieties of Class 2, f-sharp and b-flat are not in use. These latter are needed singly only for transposing the natural scales of Class 1 a major fifth higher or lower.

† The instances of two sharps or two flats divide themselves into three categories: those in which they ascend or descend (1) by fifths, after the usual manner of Western music; (2) by double fifths; or (3) by triple fifths. In these combinations it will be seen that f-sharp and b-flat have again no place.

	(1)	(2)	(3)
Signatures,	G D A E B — f c g d a D A E B f c g d	G D A E B — f c g d a A E B f g	G D A E B — f c g d a E B f c
Classes,	16 4 5 6 4 15	11 3 3 12	14 13

PART VI.—SUMMARY AND CONCLUSION.

THE foregoing pages, although they constitute, as the PREFACE informs us, a tabulation of "results" in a particular school of music rather than a treatise on music in general, touch incidentally, of necessity, a few points of Musical Grammar, or so-called "theory." In the following SUMMARY these latter points will appear somewhat more prominent because of the absence of the musical illustrations.

295. In the foregoing pages we therefore learn—

That there are thirtyone notes within the compass of an octave (Paragraphs 3 and 4).

296. That though, on the Pianoforte, those thirtyone notes are approximated only, they are capable of perfect illustration on instruments of the Violin family (Paragraph 12):

297. And that those thirtyone notes are sufficient to represent the different sounds of the Oriental scales (Paragraph 15).

298. That there are two varieties, major and minor, of each of the numeric intervals, and that the terms perfect and imperfect, or consonant and dissonant, as applied to the two fourths and the two fifths, being unnecessary, are not used in this work (Paragraphs 5, 6, and 7).

299. That calculate how we may, we are unable to produce, by other than empirical means, a true octave. In the ascending or descending series an augmented seventh is more than an octave, and a diminished ninth is less than an octave (Paragraphs 8 to 14).

300. That the normal diapason of 512 vibrations for treble c-natural * has, in practice, so sensibly sharpened, as to be more truly represented by 534·96602689536, the number derived from the *Table of Comparative Vibrations* (Paragraphs 17 and 18).

301. That the word "key" having previously been used in a mechanical sense to signify the finger levers of the pianoforte (as of other instruments), it is superseded, in musical notation, by the words *scale* and *mode* throughout this work (Paragraph 20).

302. That there are three diatonic *minor* fourth tetrachords, each with the semitonal interval in a different position from the others (Paragraph 21).

303. That two adjoined tetrachords make an octave (Paragraph 22).

304. That there is one diatonic *major* fourth tetrachord without any semitonal interval (Paragraph 23).

305. That the octaval blending of the four diatonic tetrachords induces three classes of diatonic scales, differing in the number of consecutive tones, from three to five (Paragraphs 25 to 30).

306. That the second and third classes of diatonic scales develop three *diminished* fourth tetrachords, one of which is an anticipation of the chromatic genus; while the other two, being diatonic in their origin, are credited to the diatonic genus (Paragraphs 27 and 28).

307. That the diatonic scales differ in degrees of purity (Paragraphs 38 to 42).

308. That they lend themselves readily to Double Counterpoint inversion (Paragraphs 43 to 47).

309. That the Gregorian modes, though named after the old Greek modes, differ from them in their manner of development: taking an upward progress, yet styling it a *hypo* or downward progress (Paragraphs 50 to 76).

---

* It will be useful to remember, that the proportion of the conjoint notes on the treble c-natural pianoforte key, at the normal pitch of 512 vibrations, is as follows:—

B-sharp,	518⁴⁹⁵⁹⁶
C-natural,	512
D-double-flat,	505·⁵⁷⁷⁷⁷

The proportion of the same notes in the raised pitch of the text above will be found by halving the last three lines in Paragraph 18.

SUMMARY AND CONCLUSION. 145

310. That of the sixteen diatonic scales, eight have minor thirds, and eight (of which one is unworkable) have major thirds, and are capable of being styled respectively "minor and major scales" (Paragraph 78).

311. The eight minor scales, in the decreasing order of their minority, stand thus, the intervals excepted, or not named, being major:—

No. 13 has all its intervals minor.
No. 14 has all its intervals, excepting the second, minor.
No. 1 has all its intervals, excepting the fifth, minor.
No. 3 has its second, third, fourth and seventh, minor.
No. 2 has its third, fourth, sixth and seventh, minor.
No. 7 has its second, third and fourth, minor.
No. 4 has its third, fourth and seventh, minor.
No. 8 has its third and fourth minor.

312. The seven working major scales, in the increasing order of their majority, stand thus, the intervals not named, or excepted, being minor:—

No. 15 has its second and third major.
No. 5 has its second, third and fifth, major.
No. 6 has its second, third, fifth and sixth, major.
No. 10 has its second, third, fourth and fifth, major.
No. 9 has all its intervals, excepting the fourth, major.
No. 11 has all its intervals, excepting the seventh, major.
No. 12 has all its intervals major.

313. That the semitonal interval is minor or major, according as it repeats the same scale interval, or leads to an adjoining one (Paragraph 91).

314. But it is a great misnomer thus to style them, for the minor semitone, c-natural : c-sharp, is a larger interval than the major semitone, c-natural : d-flat, as may be seen by reference to the *Table of Comparative Vibrations* in paragraph 18.

315. The lowest terms to which these two intervals can be reduced are:—

MINOR (but larger) SEMITONE, OR AUGMENTED PRIME.
497·664 : 531·441
MAJOR (but smaller) SEMITONE, OR MINOR SECOND.
497·664 : 524·288

It will thus be seen that the terms *minor* and *major*, as applied to the semitonal intervals, have regard only to their appearance on paper, and have no reference to the actual relative size of the respective intervals.

316. That a great difference exists between the doubly-augmented second and the diminished fourth, which can be explained only by a proper distribution of the above minor and major semitones (Paragraphs 91 and 94).

317. These differing intervals, though made by the pianoforte to assimilate themselves to the form of the major third, differ each in extent from that major third as well as from one another. Thus, while the doubly-augmented second is represented by:— 220·150628352 : 282·429536481
the major third, a larger interval, is represented by the reduced proportional number:—
220·150628352 : 278·628139008
and the diminished fourth, the largest nominal interval, is represented by the still further reduced proportional number:— 220·150628352 : 274·877906944

318. As we have found it necessary in paragraphs 315 and 317 to give lowest terms of five intervals, in comparative groups of two and three,* we think this a convenient place to add the lowest term of each of the

* From these comparative groups of two and three lowest terms we may learn another lesson:—that the numerals 531·441
and 524·288 represent
the two notes credited to a pianoforte black key, the sharp being above, and the flat below; while the numerals 282·429536481
278·628139008
and 274·877906944 represent
the three notes credited to a pianoforte white key, the sharp or doublesharp being above, the natural being midway, and the flat or doubleflat below.

U

practicable intervals in its separate and absolute form. It will be observed that four intervals, which are contained in the *Table of Comparative Vibrations* at paragraph 18, are, as calculated from c-natural, here not enumerated, having little practical value:—(1) the doubly-augmented prime, (2) the doubly-augmented second, (3) the doubly-augmented fifth, (4) and the doubly-augmented sixth. Also, that the diminished second (a descending interval in an ascending series, and an ascending interval in a descending series) is replaced by the diminished ninth; the introduction of which makes the opportunity for the insertion of the minor and major ninths, which, both melodially and harmonically, have a value of their own quite otherwise than as octavo duplicates of the minor and major seconds. The plus mark + shows that the second proportional numeral is in excess of what the pianoforte offers, thus denoting a larger interval: and *vice versa*, the minus mark − shows a smaller interval than on the pianoforte, caused by an excess in the first proportional numeral.

Augmented prime	2048 :	2187 +
Minor second	243 :	256 −
Major second	8 :	9 +
Augmented second	16384 :	19683 +
Diminished third	59049 :	65446 −
Minor third	27 :	32 −
Major third	64 :	81 +
Augmented third	131072 :	177147 +
Diminished fourth	6561 :	8192 −
Minor fourth	3 :	4 −
Major fourth	512 :	729 +
Augmented fourth	1048576 :	1594323 + +
Diminished fifth	1594323 :	2097152 − −
Minor fifth	729 :	1024 −
Major fifth	2 :	3 +
Augmented fifth	4096 :	6561 +
Diminished sixth	177147 :	262144 −
Minor sixth	81 :	128 −
Major sixth	16 :	27 +
Augmented sixth	32723 :	59049 +
Diminished seventh	19683 :	32768 −
Minor seventh	9 :	16 −
Major seventh	128 :	243 +
Augmented seventh	262144 :	531441 +
Diminished octave	2187 :	4096 −
Octave	1 :	2
Augmented octave	1024 :	2187 +
Diminished ninth	531441 :	1048576 −
Minor ninth	243 :	512 −
Major ninth	4 :	9 +

319. That the semi-chromatic and other scales, Nos. 17 to 36, are capable, to the small extent only of six numbers, of legitimate Double Counterpoint; but that the remaining fourteen are capable of an illegitimate species thereof, which is quite as useful in practice, though not so elegant in form, as the ordinary legitimate species (Paragraphs 95 to 98).

320. In confirmation of paragraph 99 we may say, that were it possible to utilise all the thirtyone notes within the compass of an octave for transposition of the twohundred and fiftythree chromatic scales, the number of those scales would be 7843. If to these we add the thirtysix scales of the diatonic genus treated in the same manner ($36 \times 31 = 1116$), we should have a grand total of 8959 scales.

SUMMARY AND CONCLUSION.

321. But we find in paragraph 155, that by a process of selection we utilise only onehundred and twentysix out of the (36 + 253 =) twohundred and eightynine untransposed scales. This reduced number of onehundred and twentysix scales would, however, if transposed into all the thirtyone notes of the octave, yield a total of 3906 scales.

322. If the reader will test the whole of the onehundred and twentysix selected scales in the manner applied to the first and last of the series in the next paragraph, he will find that no one of the number can be transposed into the whole thirtyone notes. The transpositions oscillate between the two extremes which follow, thus:—25, 23, 22, 21, 20, and 16; and the practical total will be found to be 2576 scales, each differing in some respects from all the others. These twothousand fivehundred and seventysix differing octave scales, however, furnish, the reader may perhaps think, sufficient ground for the development of any musical idea.

323. POSSIBLE TRANSPOSITIONS OF

SCALE No. 1.

(1)	e	f	g	a	b	c	d	e
(2)	E	F	G	A	B	C	D	E
	E	—	G	A	B	—	D	E
(3)	D	e	F	G	A	b	C	D
(4)	d	e	f	g	a	b	c	d
(5)	d	E	f	g	a	B	c	d
(6)	D	E	F	G	A	B	C	D
	D	—	—	G	A	—	—	D
(7)	C	d	e	F	G	a	b	C
(8)	c	d	e	f	g	a	b	c
(9)	c	D	E	f	g	A	B	c
(10)	C	D	E	F	G	A	B	C
(11)	b	c	d	e	F	g	a	b
(12)	b	c	d	e	f	g	a	b
(13)	B	C	D	E	f	G	A	B
	B	—	D	E	F	G	A	B
	A	b	C	D	—	F	G	A
(14)	a	b	c	d	e	f	g	a
(15)	a	B	c	d	e	f	g	a
(16)	A	B	C	D	E	F	G	A
	A	—	—	D	E	—	G	A
(17)	G	a	b	C	D	e	F	G
(18)	g	a	b	c	d	e	f	g
(19)	g	A	B	c	d	E	f	g
(20)	G	A	B	c	D	E	F	G
	G	—	—	—	D	—	—	G
(21)	F	g	a	b	C	d	e	F
(22)	f	g	a	b	c	d	e	f
(23)	f	G	A	B	c	D	E	f
(24)	F	G	A	B	C	D	E	F
(25)	e	f	g	a	b	c	d	e

SCALE No. 288.

(1)	f	g	a	b	C	d	e	f
(2)	F	g	A	B	c	d	E	F
	e	—	—	A	—	—	D	e
	e	—	F	G	a	—	C	d	e
(3)	E	f	g	a	b	c	d	E
(4)	E	f	g	A	b	c	D	E
	D	—	—	—	G	—	C	d
	d	—	—	—	G	—	C	d
(5)	d	e	F	g	A	b	c	d
(6)	D	e	f	g	a	b	c	D
(7)	D	E	f	G	a	B	c	D
	C	—	—	—	—	—	—	C
	c	D	—	F	—	A	b	c
(8)	c	d	e	f	G	a	b	c
(9)	c	d	e	f	g	a	B	c
	b	—	—	—	—	—	A	b
	b	C	D	e	—	G	a	b
(10)	B	c	d	e	F	g	a	B
(11)	B	c	d	E	f	g	A	B
	A	—	—	—	—	—	—	A
	a	—	—	D	—	—	G	a
	a	b	C	d	—	F	g	a
(12)	A	b	c	d	e	f	g	A
(13)	A	B	c	D	e	f	G	A
	G	—	—	—	—	—	—	G
	g	A	—	C	—	—	F	g
(14)	g	a	b	c	D	e	f	g
(15)	G	a	b	c	d	e	f	G*
(16)	G	A	B	c	d	E	F	G
	F	—	—	—	—	—	—	F
	f	G	A	b	—	D	e	f

* It will be seen that this g-flat transposition of the scale, which possesses one of the two simplest forms of the doubly-diminished tetrachord displayed in Examples LVI. and LXIX., possesses also the greatest number of natural notes. The reason it does not lead the CLASS 18, of which it forms a part, is, that the two accidental notes it possesses are of different grades, one flat, the other sharp. (See last sentence in Paragraphs 92, 106, &c.) The same may be said of the d-flat transposition of scale No. 283 in CLASS 17.

BYZANTINE MUSIC.

324. That the Oriental chromatic tetrachord contains two semitonal intervals, or minor seconds, so that the octave scale formed of two such tetrachords contains four semitones where the diatonic scales had two only. These four semitonal intervals necessitate the existence of two augmented seconds in the octave, which augmented seconds are the leading feature in all Oriental chromatic music (Paragraph 104).

325. The mention just made in the previous paragraph, and in paragraphs 19, 104, 247, and elsewhere, of the double allowance of major semitonal intervals, or minor seconds, in the Oriental chromatic tetrachords and scales, as compared with those of the diatonic genus, and of the consequent necessary introduction thereby into the former of a third variety of second, composed of a tone and a minor semitone, and styled *the augmented second*, makes it desirable to present the chromatic scale divided into the whole of its component intervals, after the manner of the diatonic scale in Example I. We give it in the normal scale of c-natural with flats, for better comparison with Example I. Our readers will notice that modern composers are indebted to the Oriental chromatic scale for some of the reputed novelties which distinguish their works, as, for instance, *the diminished seventh** (the correlative of the augmented second), so largely used by the well-known "romantic school" of Germany ;† *the augmented sixth*,‡ known by its varied accompanying notes as the French, German, and Italian sixth; and *the augmented fifth*,§ so already nearly done to death by followers of the distinguished French composer, M. Gounod.

EXAMPLE CXCVIII.

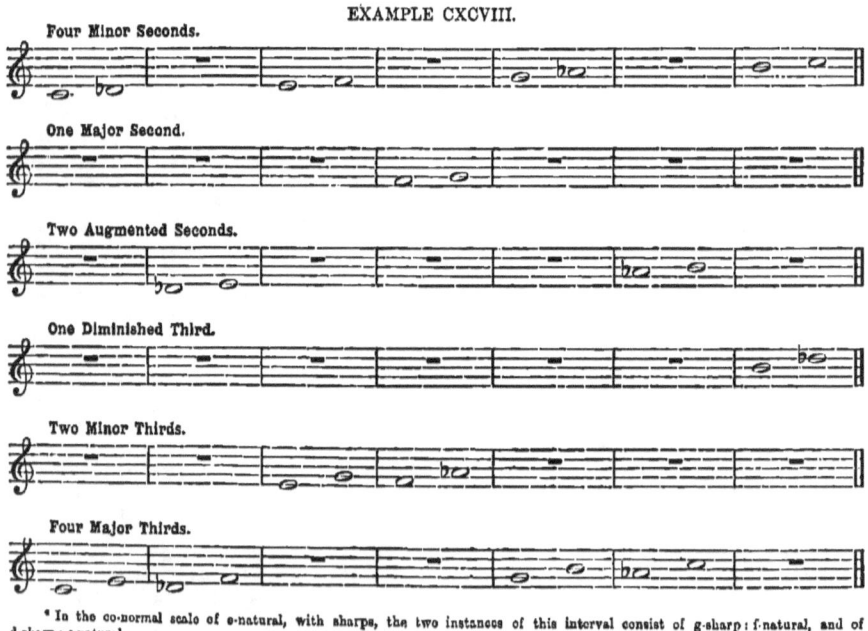

* In the co-normal scale of e-natural, with sharps, the two instances of this interval consist of g-sharp : f-natural, and of d-sharp : c-natural.
† Beethoven is reported to have said of Weber's poetic Opera *Euryanthe*, that it was "a collection of diminished sevenths."
‡ In the co-normal scale of e-natural, with sharps, this interval consists of f-natural : d-sharp.
§ In the co-normal scale of e-natural, with sharps, this interval consists of c-natural : g-sharp.

SUMMARY AND CONCLUSION.

326. That the favourite Minor scale of the present day, No. 44, styled in Example CVI. *The Chromatic Hypodorian Mode*, with its minor sixth and major seventh, is an outcome of the Oriental system, being a mixture of the diatonic with the chromatic genus* (Paragraphs 106 and 107).

327. That while the octave scale of the chromatic genus develops two major fourth tetrachords against one in the diatonic genus (Paragraph 111):

328. It gives us but one instance of the diminished fourth tetrachord to two in the diatonic genus (Paragraph 117). This one chromatic diminished fourth tetrachord was, as we have seen in paragraphs 27, 117, and 306, first developed by the diatonic genus.

329. That the onehundred and eight chromatic scales thus far recorded divide themselves into two distinct orders: (1) pure, (2) mixed (Paragraph 124).

330. That of the onehundred and fortyfour diatonic and chromatic scales, eighteen are unworkable, thus reducing the number of practical scales to onehundred and twentysix (Paragraphs 125 to 127).

331. That while fiftysix of those onehundred and twentysix working scales contain in their internal incidence none other than the twelve diatonic and chromatic tetrachords, the remaining seventy scales† are not so happily framed, but develop fourteen non-fundamental tetrachords (Paragraphs 128 to 130).

332. That of these fourteen non-fundamental tetrachords, five only are worthy of retention, and constitute a compound genus: (1) the four additional major fourth tetrachords, and (2) the one instance of the doubly-diminished fourth tetrachord (Paragraphs 131 and 136).

333. These five additional tetrachords introduce us to fortytwo new scales needed to complete the ten classes or families of the former series to which they are allied. The nine rejected non-fundamental tetrachords govern also fortytwo scales of the former series. By removing these latter fortytwo scales with their undesirable internal incidence, we make room for the former, and still preserve the number of one hundred and twentysix working scales (Paragraphs 150 to 152).

334. That the onehundred and twentysix selected working scales form eighteen classes or families of scales, with seven instances each (Paragraph 152).

335. These eighteen classes or families of scales being analysed and detailed in paragraphs 157 to 195, we have nothing to add thereto. But the following sample scale from each of the classes on the tonal level of the first or *Dorian Mode*,‡ will, we think, be of interest.

EXAMPLE CXCIX.

---

* In paragraphs 79, and 310 to 312, we give the list of minor and major scales in the earlier part of the diatonic genus. It may be as well to state that besides these there are, in the remaining onehundred and eleven working scales of paragraph 155, no fewer than 43 scales with minor thirds, making a total of 51 minor scales; and 42 scales with major thirds, making a total of 49 major scales. Sixteen of the residue have diminished thirds, and ten have augmented thirds, but both these groups are external to the modern classification.

† Of those seventy, twofifths only, twentyeight in all, are ultimately retained.

‡ We purposely use the words "*tonal level* of the Dorian mode," because several of the scales in this example, notably those with the fundamental major fourth tetrachord, could by no possibility be styled even Pseudo-Dorian. Some with the fundamental minor fourth tetrachord are already otherwise denominated: *e.g.*, No. 37 is a *Hyper Chromatic Hypodorian;* No. 38 is a co-normal *Hyper Chromatic Lydian;* and No. 39 is a co-normal *Hyper Chromatic Hypolydian.* See Example CVI.

SUMMARY AND CONCLUSION. 151

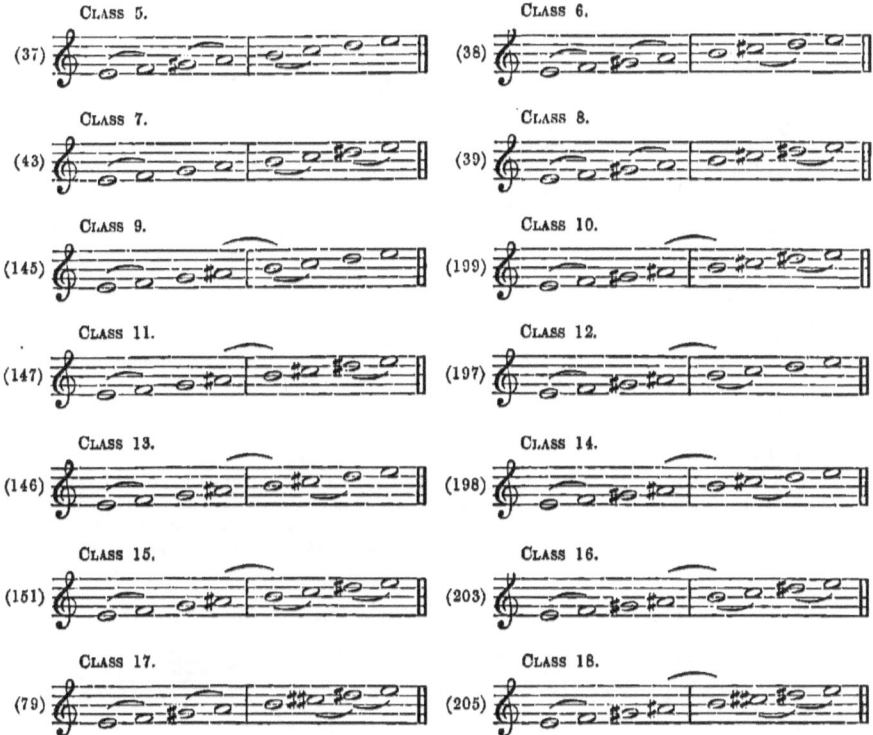

336. It will be observed that the above sample scales could have been set out in f-natural or b-natural, the other two of three common notes, on the tonal level of the Hypolydian or Mixolydian modes. Our readers will long ere this have learned that these modes have not the pre-eminence attaching to the Dorian mode: hence our preference for the latter. But it will be a useful exercise, if the reader chooses, to set himself the task of laying out other examples of like nature with the above, on the tonal level of those two modes. After which he may proceed to the tonal level of each of the other modes: but for these he will need occasionally to use the ordinary artifices of transposition.

337. That certain of the mixed diatonic and chromatic scales, having the lower tetrachord diatonic, are numbered with the eight tones as a chromatic variety: while certain, having the lower tetrachord chromatic, form a Hyper chromatic variety (Paragraph 196).

338. That the untransposed chromatic scales possess no d-natural, the most fertile note of the diatonic genus (Paragraph 197).

339. That Oriental music, especially of the olden time, as the product of a simple nature, is, of necessity, also simple (Paragraph 199).

152   BYZANTINE MUSIC.

340. Comment on the ancient and modern specimens thereof given will be found in paragraphs 200 to 281. These comments, it is hoped, are sufficiently explicit to give the reader a fair idea of the peculiarities of the Eastern musical mind. The specimens given are gathered from the thirteen following sources:—

(1) Balakireff's *Sbornik Rooskikh Narodnikh Peysen*: Examples CVIII., CXIX., CXX., CXXI., CXXVIII., CXXXII., CXXXIV., CXXXV., CXXXIX., CXLIV., CXLV.
(2) Traditional Russian Church use: Examples CIX., CX., CLI., CLII.
(3) Oratoriette *Baptism*:* Example CXI.
(4) Bourgault-Ducoudray's *Trente Melodies Populaires de Grèce et d'Orient*: Examples CXII., CXXVI., CXXXI., CXLI., CXLVI., CLIII., CLIV., CLXIX., CLXX., CLXXII., CLXXVI., CLXXVII., CLXXXII., CLXXXVIII., CXCII., CXCIII.
(5) The *Scottish Review* on Rev. Jules Blin's *Chants Liturgiques des Coptes*:* Examples CXIII., CXXXIII., CCVIII.
(6) Traditional Greek Church use, from Rev. Dr. Neale's *Hymns of the Eastern Church*:* Example CXVIII.
(7) Naumann's *History of Music*: Example CXXVII.
(8) *Aria Patetica*:* Example CLVIII.
(9) Tchouhadjian's Opera *Leblebidji Hor-hor Agha*: Examples CLX., CLXXVIII.
(10) Guatelli's 24 *Arie nazionali e Canti popolari Orientali*: Examples CLXI., CLXII., CLXIII., CLXVII., CLXXI., CLXXXI., CLXXXII., CLXXXIII., CXCVI., CC.
(11) Christ and Paranakis' *Anthologia Græca Carminum Christianorum*: Example CLXXXVII.
(12) *Specimens of Ancient Byzantine Ecclesiastical Melody*:* Example CCII.
(13) *Osmanié Imperial March*: Example CCIV.

341. In footnote †, at page 103, we allude to the rhythm of the sevenfold or septuple measure, but the Specimens in PART V. furnish no instance of the measure. We think it right to supply the omission, as all Eastern peoples are very fond of this rhythmic form, and as Western composers occasionally show their appreciation of it.† We are again indebted to a talented member of the Imperial family at Constantinople for a very fine example.

EXAMPLE CC.
MELODY OF RAFIE SULTANA, DAUGHTER OF THE LATE SULTAN.‡

* These five are publications of the present Writer.   † Berlioz has a notable instance in the "Incantation music" at pp. 28-31 of his Trilogy *The Childhood of* CHRIST (London: Forsyth, Brothers); but the editor has unfortunately divided the 7/4 measures into alternate measures of 3/4 and 4/4 rhythm, thereby adding nothing either to the clearness of the Composer, or to the ease of his readers.
‡ Guatelli, Series I., No. 5. Transposed a minor fourth higher.

SUMMARY AND CONCLUSION. 153

342. We have left it to the student to supply the harmony in this example, which he will find a not very difficult task, as the melody is practically in the now popular form of the Minor mode, with minor sixth and major seventh, and in the universal Major mode. The Minor mode takes the co-normal form of *The Hyper Chromatic Hypodorian Mode*, of which it utilizes six notes, with an external lower note; while the Major mode takes the authentic form of *The Lydian Mode*, of which it utilizes also six notes, with an external lower note.

EXAMPLE CCI.

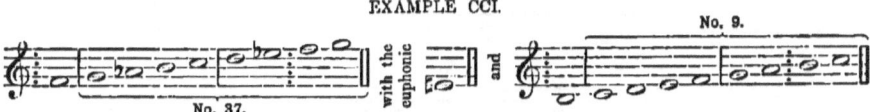

The melody divides itself into four periods of four measures each, of which periods the second and fourth are similar, as are also the second section of the first and third. The measures themselves, unequally though they divide (1, 2, 3, 4 : 1, 2, 3), form each a complete phrase; but the phrases in periods 2 and 4 are very compactly joined, so compactly, indeed, as to form a continuous stream of notes. The *ad libitum* small beat-notes, placed for convenience at the commencement of the example, are, of course, not included in this measural reckoning, not being a portion of the melody proper.

343. In CONCLUSION we present two specimens of greater length and importance than any we have yet given: (1) a portion of an ancient chromatic setting, in great repute, of the Lenten and longer Liturgy of the Greek Church, contained in *Specimens of Ancient Byzantine Ecclesiastical Melody, according to the use of the Great Church of Christ in Constantinople* (London: Augener & Co., 1879); and (2) a modern application to military purposes of the same chromatic genus.* The first of these specimens is as follows:—

EXAMPLE CCII.

* The copy here followed was made by us many years ago in Turkey, but whether from a printed edition or MS. our memory is not certain. Many different musical gems were copied by us during our different periods of research, and the greater number of the originals were in MS.

CONCLUSION.

344. The melody of the foregoing is constructed, in the main, in *The Pure Chromatic Mode*, with an admixture of *The Hypolydian Mode* transposed a major fifth lower; but is printed without signature to impress its chromaticism more plainly, and to make its vocalisation more sure.

EXAMPLE CCIII.

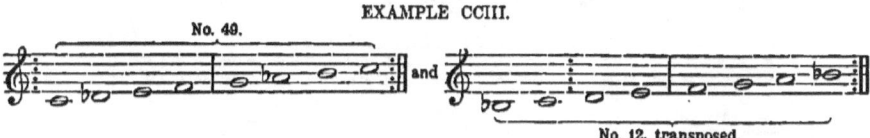

345. The student, in setting four part vocal harmony to these Oriental chromatic melodies, will at once feel the difficulty caused by the augmented second of the chromatic scale. However freely that interval may be used in the melody, as in the present instance, where it occurs twelve times in descending and ten times in ascending, it cannot be introduced with the same freedom in the accompanying parts on account of the uncertainty of its attack by the average choralist, singing without instrumental assistance. The minor second and minor sixth of the scale can be utilized whenever other than the major third and major seventh are immediate neighbours: but when these latter exist, the second and sixth become almost of necessity major also. Hence it will be seen in the above Example CCII., that the augmented second occurs in the accompanying parts once only, in a short imitation passage (made all the easier by its being an imitation) at bar 18, which may be regarded as a small acknowledgment of the modal claim: while the a-flat and d-flat are used freely enough whenever contact with b-natural and e-natural could be avoided. The two transposed Hypolydian phrases of four and a half measures each, commencing with bars 19 and 28, afford an excuse for anticipating the harmony of that transposed mode, with its b-flat, on the four and a half measures commencing with the second half of bar 8: a very convenient and justifiable means of avoiding, for these latter measures' length, the difficulty of the previously alluded to augmented second.

346. Our second concluding specimen, well known and appreciated in other as well as Turkish official and military circles, is the following, which, like Example CCII., we print without signature.

v 2

EXAMPLE CCIV.
OSMANIE IMPERIAL MARCH, FOR THE PIANOFORTE.

CONCLUSION.

347. This fine March, being an instrumental piece, can venture on what would be out of place, or even impracticable, in a vocal composition. The melody is constructed of twentyfour differing notes, which aggregated, stand thus:—

EXAMPLE CCV.

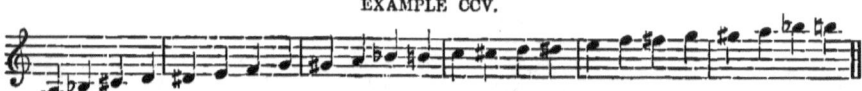

These notes, when separated, furnish us with three classes of scales: (1) *The Chromatic and Hyper Chromatic Hypodorian Mode*, transposed; (2) *The Pure Chromatic Mode*, transposed; and (3) a resolution into its normal pitch of *The Hyper Chromatic Hypodorian Mode*.

EXAMPLE CCVI.

CONCLUSION.   159

A considerable effect is produced by the judicious use of the three different euphonic notes which stand external to the scales. We will now take a short glance at the treatment of the different periods in this March.

348. The first period, of eight bars, though it passes, at the end of its first performance, into the dominant of the principal or *Chromatic Hypodorian Mode*, closes in the principal mode at the repeat. It is in this first period that we experience the first effect of the euphonic g-sharp and d-sharp, and few can be found to other than enjoy that effect.

349. The second period, of twelve bars, is in two distinct modes: (1) *The Pure Chromatic Mode*, transposed, at bars 1 to 5, and 8; and (2) the normal *Hyper Chromatic Hypodorian Mode* at bars 6, 7, and 9 to 12. In this period we notice the vagueness alluded to in paragraph 249, caused by the absence of the third from the accompanying left hand measures, which vague accompaniment, though intended merely to represent the beating of the small side-drum, adds much to the mystery of the chromatic melody careering above. This side-drum accompaniment in the first bars of the repeat is led in by the final bar of the first performance. The last four bars of this period stamp the whole piece with the brand of modernism, in spite of the euphonic d-sharp, which aims at giving it a chromatic connection by inducing an augmented second with the adjoining c-natural.

350. The third and double period of sixteen bars reverts to the original *Chromatic Hypodorian Modes*, both authentic and plagal, and occupies the whole of the thirteen notes assigned to them in Example CCVI. The reader will have observed that the dominant or fifth of the original mode has been very conspicuous thus far. The first performance of the first period closed in A, the dominant mode of D. The second period was entirely constructed of two forms of A scales: *The Pure Chromatic Mode*, transposed; and a plagal form of the favourite "Minor Mode," or *Hyper Chromatic Hypodorian*. The present third period takes up the harmonic parable with a dominant seventh of the original mode, and that harmony prevails over rather more than one half of the remaining 42 bar measures. This is not at all in the old manner, but reminds one of the satirical remark of the great Handel applied by him to the popular music of his day, in which tonal and dominant harmonies chiefly prevailed:—" Now Dees are trumps, gentlemen; now Ayes." The old musicians preferred, as may be seen in nearly every instance of the chromatic genus quoted by us, to pass into the subdominant: so extensively, indeed, that many persons think the subdominant to be the real fundamental tonic. The contrary preference for the dominant in the present March shows the strong influence of modern ideas in the composer's mind; which ideas are, however, found to consist with a considerable and hearty appreciation of the chromatic genus. For we see the subdominant manner happily preserved in the final eight bars of the present and next following periods. And there are no external euphonic notes to take our attention in this third and double period of sixteen bars.

351. The chief noticeable feature in the fourth period is that it consists of fourteen bar measures. It is thus a double period, but divides unequally, into six and eight bars respectively. The first portion, of six bars, consists of two contracted sections of three bars each, which are evidently a variant of the similarly situated sections in the previous period. They commence in the same manner, and abound in the same dominant harmony, but are scarcely so pleasing, the mind being conscious of the doubly occurring rhythmical deficiency. The second portion, of eight bars, with the subdominant tendency, is identical with that in the previous period, to which we have already alluded in paragraph 350. This present double period, unlike the previous one, is repeated in performance; but like it, possesses no euphonic notes.

352. The modern character to which we have already directed attention by means of two particulars, is confirmed beyond possibility of cavil by the fifth or Codetta period of twelve bars, at which we now arrive. The opening four bars, with their Western chromatic semitonal rise, involving the euphonic d-sharp and f-sharp, familiar though they seem to us, must have startled Eastern ears when first presented to them. But the eight bars which follow those four, excepting that the dominant harmony proclaims their modern construction, are sufficiently Oriental in character, and tended, we may hope, to restore the Oriental equanimity. That the whole piece is now of universal acceptance with all Ottoman subjects is due to the fact of its general excellence, and to the further fact that use reconciles all of us, Easterns and Westerns, to many inconsistencies. In the two final bars the shake on the augmented second, b-flat and c-sharp, is sufficiently noteworthy to justify the attention of the reader.

353. In the edition followed in preparation of the present copy of this March, we are directed after the Codetta

to begin again, and proceed until we reach the word FINE immediately previous to the Codetta. This is to play the whole piece, excepting the Codetta, twice over, which makes a total (including repeats) of 176 bars. But our own experience of the piece, in which we are borne out by the approval of many friends of Turkish allegiance, has suggested that it is better, rather than stop at the word FINE, to proceed again to the Codetta, and then return to the first or leading period, finishing thereat and therewith. This addition of 28 bars in performance will raise the number from 176 to 204: a small increase of labour and time for which the increase of effect far more than compensates.

POSTSCRIPT.

354. Our work was brought to a close by the above Turkish Imperial March of the Osmanié. But a friend, whose advice is highly valued, subsequently called attention to the fact that the Anaphoral "Améns" in the twice quoted Coptic Liturgy of St. Basil are very characteristic, and suggested their insertion. In complying with this suggestion, we feel that we are not only furnishing a small addition of considerable practical value, but are also making the best possible conclusion to our treatise. For every action of our lives, whether secular or religious, ought to permit of the postulate or desire—Γένοιτο, Be it so, Amén.

355. In the first Coptic expression below, uttered by the Priest, we find a "ph" as well as an "f." But they must not be assimilated in pronunciation. The "ph" must be treated as two distinct letters, as they are in the word she*ph*erd; not as an "f," as twice in *ph*ilosopher. Also we call attention to the fact that the word "Amén" is, in all Eastern languages, pronounced with the long sound of ή, as in "Ameen," which is the form of transliteration adopted by Mr. Lane and other writers.

356. Of the three following instances, we have, in the first, the fivefold leading measure, of the rhythm 1, 2: 1, 2, 3, of Examples CXLV. and CLIV., very pleasingly imitated by the Alto answer in the fifth below of the Soprano subject; which subject and answer joined together, being each a diatonic tetrachord, form a diatonic octave scale, No. 9, the scale of the 3rd Tone, or *The Lydian Mode* (Paragraphs 22 and 73).

EXAMPLE CCVII.

357. There remains now only to call attention to the cheerful but quaint Hypodorian effect of the triple "Amén" in the third and last instance, and to commend the use of that third and last instance to clergymen, choirmasters, and others, as an appropriate *finale* to any religious function.

EXAMPLE CCVIII.
FROM THE COPTIC LITURGY OF ST. BASIL, FOR FOUR VOICES.

POSTSCRIPT. 161

ΤΕΛΟΣ.

ERRATA.

Page 23, paragraph 66, line 2, place a colon after—plagal:
" 25, footnote, line 1, for "Baritone" read—Barytone
" 26, paragraph 80, line 3, cancel apostrophe after—*Series*
" 27, paragraph 85, line 1, place a colon after—great:
" 27, paragraph 85, line 2, place a semicolon after—inversion;
" 29, scale (18), add a second flat before the third note—B
" 31, paragraph 94, line 3, after "above" add—in paragraph 91
" 33, paragraph 100, lines 2 and 3, cancel apostrophe after—series
" 57, scale (246), for "d" read—*d*
" 70, paragraph 169, line 1, for "LXXVII." read—LXXVIII.
" 86, footnote, line 1, for "observe" read—notice
" 87, paragraph 206, line 3, for "diatonic" read—authentic
" 97, Greek text, line 1, for "$\chi\iota$" read—$\chi\upsilon$
" 112, footnote, for "normal" read—co-normal
" 132, stave 4, bar 1, remove the second repeat (c) with its attendant dots, and place them at commencement of bar 3.

www.ingramcontent.com/pod-product-compliance
Lightning Source LLC
Chambersburg PA
CBHW030434190426
43202CB00036B/549